THE CARPATHO-RUSYN AMERICANS

The Peoples of North America

THE CARPATHO-RUSYN AMERICANS

Paul Robert Magocsi

CHELSEA HOUSE PUBLISHERS

New York   Philadelphia

On the cover: Members of SS. Peter and Paul Church, Struthers, Ohio, in costume before a performance of the annual Nativity play, 1925.

Chelsea House Publishers
Editor-in-Chief: Nancy Toff
Executive Editor: Remmel T. Nunn
Managing Editor: Karyn Gullen Browne
Copy Chief: Juliann Barbato
Picture Editor: Adrian G. Allen
Art Director: Maria Epes
Manufacturing Manager: Gerald Levine

19461755

The Peoples of North America
Senior Editor: Sean Dolan

Staff for THE CARPATHO-RUSYN AMERICANS
Assistant Editor: James M. Cornelius
Copy Editor: Philip Koslow
Deputy Copy Chief: Nicole Bowen
Editorial Assistant: Elizabeth Nix
Picture Research: PAR/NYC
Assistant Art Director: Loraine Machlin
Senior Designer: Noreen M. Lamb
Production Coordinator: Joseph Romano
Cover Illustration: Paul Biniasz
Banner Design: Hrana L. Janto

First Printing

1 3 5 7 9 8 6 4 2

Library of Congress Cataloging-in-Publication Data
Magocsi, Paul R.
  The Carpatho-Rusyn Americans / Paul Robert Magocsi.
    p.   cm. — (Peoples of North America)
  Bibliography: p.
  Includes index.
  Summary: Discusses the history, culture, and religion of the Carpatho-Rusyns, factors encouraging their emigration to North America, and their acceptance as an ethnic group there.
  ISBN 0-87754-866-8
      0-7910-0283-7 (pbk.)
  1. Ruthenian Americans—Juvenile literature.   [1. Ruthenian Americans.]   I. Title.   II. Series.   89-7173
E184.U5M32   1989   CIP
973'.0491791—dc20   AC

CONTENTS

THE PEOPLES OF NORTH AMERICA

CHELSEA HOUSE PUBLISHERS

A NATION
OF NATIONS

Daniel Patrick Moynihan

The Constitution of the United States begins: "We the People of the United States . . ." Yet, as we know, the United States is not made up of a single group of people. It is made up of many peoples. Immigrants from Europe, Asia, Africa, and Central and South America settled in North America seeking a new life filled with opportunities unavailable in their homeland. Coming from many nations, they forged one nation and made it their own. More than 100 years ago, Walt Whitman expressed this perception of America as a melting pot: "Here is not merely a nation, but a teeming Nation of nations."

Although the ingenuity and acts of courage of these immigrants, our ancestors, shaped the North American way of life, we sometimes take their contributions for granted. This fine series, *The Peoples of North America*, examines the experiences and contributions of the immigrants and how these contributions determined the future of the United States and Canada.

Immigrants did not abandon their ethnic traditions when they reached the shores of North America. Each ethnic group had its own customs and traditions, and each brought different experiences, accomplishments, skills, values, styles of dress, and tastes in food that lingered long after its arrival. Yet this profusion of differences created a singularity, or bond, among the immigrants.

The United States and Canada are unusual in this respect. Whereas religious and ethnic differences have sparked intolerance throughout the rest of the world—from the 17th-century religious wars to the 19th-century nationalist movements in Europe to the near extermination of the Jewish people under Nazi Germany—North Americans have struggled to learn how to respect each other's differences and live in harmony.

Millions of immigrants from scores of homelands brought diversity to our continent. In a mass migration, some 12 million immigrants passed through the waiting rooms of New York's Ellis Island; thousands more came to the West Coast. At first, these immigrants were welcomed because labor was needed to meet the demands of the Industrial Age. Soon, however, the new immigrants faced the prejudice of earlier immigrants who saw them as a burden on the economy. Legislation was passed to limit immigration. The Chinese Exclusion Act of 1882 was among the first laws closing the doors to the promise of America. The Japanese were also effectively excluded by this law. In 1924, Congress set immigration quotas on a country-by-country basis.

Such prejudices might have triggered war, as they did in Europe, but North Americans chose negotiation and compromise instead. This determination to resolve differences peacefully has been the hallmark of the peoples of North America.

The remarkable ability of Americans to live together as one people was seriously threatened by the issue of slavery. It was a symptom of growing intolerance in the world. Thousands of settlers from the British Isles had arrived in the colonies as indentured servants, agreeing to work for a specified number of years on farms or as apprentices in return for passage to America and room and board. When the first Africans arrived in the then-British colonies during the 17th century, some colonists thought that they too should be treated as indentured servants. Eventually, the question of whether the Africans should be viewed as indentured, like the English, or as slaves who could be owned for life, was considered in a Maryland court. The court's calamitous decree held that blacks were slaves bound to lifelong servitude, and so were their children. America went through a time of moral examination and civil war before it finally freed African slaves and their descendants. The principle that all people are created equal had faced its greatest challenge and survived.

Yet the court ruling that set blacks apart from other races fanned flames of discrimination that burned long after slavery was abolished—and that still flicker today. The concept of racism had existed for centuries in countries throughout the world. For instance, when the Manchus conquered China in the 13th century, they decreed that Chinese and Manchus could not intermarry. To impress their superiority on the conquered Chinese, the Manchus ordered all Chinese men to wear their hair in a long braid called a queue.

By the 19th century, some intellectuals took up the banner of racism, citing Charles Darwin. Darwin's scientific studies hypothesized that highly evolved animals were dominant over other animals. Some advocates of this theory applied it to humans, asserting that certain races were more highly evolved than others and thus were superior.

This philosophy served as the basis for a new form of discrimination, not only against nonwhite people but also against various ethnic groups. Asians faced harsh discrimination and were depicted by popular 19th-century newspaper cartoonists as depraved, degenerate, and deficient in intelligence. When the Irish flooded American cities to escape the famine in Ireland, the cartoonists caricatured the typical "Paddy" (a common term for Irish immigrants) as an apelike creature with jutting jaw and sloping forehead.

By the 20th century, racism and ethnic prejudice had given rise to virulent theories of a Northern European master race. When Adolf Hitler came to power in Germany in 1933, he popularized the notion of Aryan supremacy. *Aryan*, a term referring to the Indo-European races, was applied to so-called superior physical characteristics such as blond hair, blue eyes, and delicate facial features. Anyone with darker and heavier features was considered inferior. Buttressed by these theories, the German Nazi state from

1933 to 1945 set out to destroy European Jews, along with Poles, Russians, and other groups considered inferior. It nearly succeeded. Millions of these people were exterminated.

The tragedies brought on by ethnic and racial intolerance throughout the world demonstrate the importance of North America's efforts to create a society free of prejudice and inequality.

A relatively recent example of the New World's desire to resolve ethnic friction nonviolently is the solution the Canadians found to a conflict between two ethnic groups. A long-standing dispute as to whether Canadian culture was properly English or French resurfaced in the mid-1960s, dividing the peoples of the French-speaking Quebec Province from those of the English-speaking provinces. Relations grew tense, then bitter, then violent. The Royal Commission on Bilingualism and Biculturalism was established to study the growing crisis and to propose measures to ease the tensions. As a result of the commission's recommendations, all official documents and statements from the national government's capital at Ottawa are now issued in both French and English, and bilingual education is encouraged.

The year 1980 marked a coming of age for the United States's ethnic heritage. For the first time, the U.S. Census asked people about their ethnic background. Americans chose from more than 100 groups, including French Basque, Spanish Basque, French Canadian, Afro-American, Peruvian, Armenian, Chinese, and Japanese. The ethnic group with the largest response was English (49.6 million). More than 100 million Americans claimed ancestors from the British Isles, which includes England, Ireland, Wales, and Scotland. There were almost as many Germans (49.2 million) as English. The Irish-American population (40.2 million) was third, but the next largest ethnic group, the Afro-Americans, was a distant fourth (21 million). There was a sizable group of French ancestry (13 million), as well as of Italian (12 million). Poles, Dutch, Swedes, Norwegians, and Russians followed. These groups, and other smaller ones, represent the wondrous profusion of ethnic influences in North America.

Canada, too, has learned more about the diversity of its population. Studies conducted during the French/English conflict showed that Canadians were descended from Ukrainians, Germans, Italians, Chinese, Japanese, native Indians, and Eskimos, among others. Canada found it had no ethnic majority, although nearly half of its immigrant population had come from the British Isles. Canada, like the United States, is a land of immigrants for whom mutual tolerance is a matter of reason as well as principle.

The people of North America are the descendants of one of the greatest migrations in history. And that migration is not over. Koreans, Vietnamese, Nicaraguans, Cubans, and many others are heading for the shores of North America in large numbers. This mix of cultures shapes every aspect of our lives. To understand ourselves, we must know something about our diverse ethnic ancestry. Nothing so defines the North American nations as the motto on the Great Seal of the United States: *E Pluribus Unum*— Out of Many, One.

The family of Michael and Suzanna Petruschak Petro, photographed in 1920, in Sykesville, Pennsylvania. They came to America before World War I from Zemplyn County in what is now northeastern Hungary.

FROM A LITTLE-KNOWN LAND

As drivers wind their way along the interstate highways and smaller roads of the cities and suburbs of the industrial northeastern United States, they frequently pass by churches with brightly painted golden domes that strike the viewer with their strange, onionlike shape and glistening color. These are Eastern Christian churches, and many were built and are still attended by a little-known group of people called Carpatho-Rusyns.

The Carpatho-Rusyns (pronounced Kar-PAY-tho ROOS-ins) are part of the Slavic branch of European peoples. For the most part, those who came to America did so during the two decades prior to the outbreak of World War I in 1914. Their homeland, Carpathian Rus' (or Carpatho-Ruthenia), rests along the slopes of the Carpathian Mountains and today is divided into lands ruled by three countries: Czechoslovakia, Poland, and the Soviet Union. In their European homeland and in the New World, the Carpatho-Rusyns have at times also been called Rusnaks, Ruthenians, Lemkos, Carpatho-Russians, and Carpatho-Ukrainians. Those who immigrated to the United States were particularly

Central Europe in 1914. The land historically inhabited by the Carpatho-Rusyns (at times it was called Carpathian Rus', Ruthenia, and Carpatho-Ukraine) has often fallen victim to the national ambitions of its more powerful neighbors. The people themselves (also known as Rusnaks, Lemkos, and Ruthenians) have sometimes had to adapt their ways to conciliate their rulers.

likely to be misidentified, as few American immigration officials were familiar with Carpathian Rus'.

The use of various names to identify Carpatho-Rusyns has often made it difficult to determine just how many came to the United States and Canada and how many descendants of those immigrants still live in North America. For instance, the United States Census Bureau decided that the 1980 census would list Americans of Carpatho-Rusyn background as Russians, even though the report admitted it would have been more correct to treat them as a distinct ethnic and cultural group. Although concrete statistics on Carpatho-Rusyns in the United States are still hard to come by, scholars who have studied the group conclude that today there are about 700,000 Americans who claim one or more Carpatho-Rusyn ancestors. Perhaps one-third of this number are completely Carpatho-Rusyn in ancestry. Those descendants of immigrants who married outside of their own group chose partners mainly from Americans of other Eastern-European descent—Slovaks, Poles, or Hungarians, for example. Much of their native-born tradition was thereby carried on in a semblance of its original cultural form. Like most of the Carpatho-Rusyn immigrants who came to these shores in the decades just before and after the turn of the 20th century, the second-, third-, and fourth-generation descendants tend to live in three states of the industrial Northeast: Pennsylvania, New York, and New Jersey. Others live elsewhere in the Northeast—Connecticut and Vermont—or near the Great Lakes, in Ohio and Illinois. In recent years, others have joined the migration to the Sun Belt states of Florida and California. No matter where they reside, Carpatho-Rusyns continue to provide the manpower and management for American industry.

Although the group may be little known to the larger public, some of its sons and daughters have played an important role in the history of Eastern Christianity in the United States. And a few others, including the pop artist Andy Warhol and the actress Sandra Dee, have become widely celebrated symbols of the American way of life.

THE HOMELAND

The Carpatho-Rusyn homeland is literally in the heart of Europe. Extending from the coasts of Ireland in the west all the way to the Ural Mountains, Europe reaches farther east than most North Americans realize. The continent's precise center is the little Carpatho-Rusyn village of Dilove, which is now in the Soviet Union. In 1875 and again in 1977, monuments were erected there to mark the geographic midpoint of the European continent.

The most characteristic element of Carpathian Rus' is its mountainous terrain. The north-central ranges of the Carpathian Mountains, where Rusyns live, average 2,000 feet in elevation. Covered with forests and lined with narrow, arable valleys, the entire region is very similar to the Green Mountains of Vermont. From the very beginning of their settlement in this area in the 6th and 7th centuries, Carpatho-Rusyns have lived in small villages that in many cases are home to no more than a few hundred inhabitants, and they have practiced those livelihoods most suited to a mountain people—sheepherding, logging, and small-scale agriculture. As industrialization has never taken hold in the area, the rural environment, basic economy, and way of life have remained essentially unchanged, even in the late 20th century.

Because Carpatho-Rusyns live in the very center of Europe, it is not surprising that they have been profoundly influenced by both the East and the West. Their language, for instance, is an East-Slavic dialect and is written in the Cyrillic alphabet, which was developed by the followers of Saint Cyril, the 9th-century Christian missionary, who with his brother Methodius brought Christianity to the Slavs. This means Carpatho-Rusyn is grammatically and etymologically related to the other East-Slavic languages—Russian, Byelorussian, and in particular Ukrainian. (Most modern linguists consider Carpatho-Rusyn speech to be a dialect of Ukrainian.) On the other hand, living as they have for many centuries in close proximity to the West-Slavic peoples—Poles and Slovaks—and the non-Slavic Hungarians, the Carpatho-Rusyn people's speech has been heavily influenced by these languages as well.

Between East and West

The great traditions of both the East and the West also shape Carpatho-Rusyn religious life. Like the other East Slavs, the Carpatho-Rusyns received Christianity from the Eastern Roman Empire, also called the Byzantine Empire. For centuries the Christian world had two capitals, Rome in the west and Constantinople in the east. (Today Constantinople is called Istanbul and is the largest city in the nation of Turkey.) When doctrinal differences over the spiritual and temporal authority of the pope led to a split in the church in 1054, Constantinople became the center of the Eastern, or Orthodox, Christian world, while the Western Catholic church was governed by Rome. Living as they have for centuries under the rule of countries that were officially Roman Catholic, namely Hungary and Poland, Carpatho-Rusyns were continually influenced by the Western Christian church, so much so that in 1596 and 1646 several of their bishops officially united them with Rome. The union was somewhat less than complete, however, which would later create a problem.

In the realm of politics and secular culture, Carpatho-Rusyns have again been influenced by their geographic location on the borderline between (Orthodox) East and (Roman Catholic) West. Straddling this border, Carpatho-Rusyns have functioned easily within and have picked up traits from those societies that have ruled their homeland—Hungary, Poland, and more recently Czechoslovakia. Yet they have also remained close to the Ukrainian and Russian traditions, to which they are related by linguistic and religious custom. These mutual influences are graphically revealed in Carpatho-Rusyn family names. The names are easily distinguishable in the Slavic world because of the high percentage that are similar to Hungarian names or are slavicized forms of Hungarian, such as Kovach, Lukach, Mihaly (or Mihalik), Pap, Shereghy, and Takach.

To be so affected by various political and cultural influences is common for a national or ethnic minority living in a borderland region. In this sense, Carpatho-Rusyns know very well the feeling of anguish and diminished identity that accompanies the cultural and historical partitioning that has been the fate of so many European national or ethnic minorities. For Carpatho-Rusyns, however, who have not been united in a single province, kingdom, or nation for nearly a thousand years, the sense of being at the mercy of others is more acute.

A national or ethnic minority is a group of people with its own distinct language and culture. The group usually inhabits a definable territory, but it does not have its own nation-state. For example, Welsh and Scottish minorities live within Great Britain; France is home to the Breton, the Alsatian, and some of the Basque minorities. In eastern and central Europe the comparatively large number of national minorities have had to learn the brutal lesson that stronger powers do not always heed their requests for autonomy. Since World War II, the territory of the Carpatho-Rusyns has lain within the borders of the Soviet Union, Czechoslovakia, and Poland.

Being ruled by others is not a recent development for the Carpatho-Rusyns. Their lands have from earliest times attracted the attention of both eastern and western political powers. When the representatives of the first organized state structures in the area began to reach the Carpathian Mountains in the 11th and 12th centuries, Rusyns came under the influence of three medieval powers: Roman Catholic Hungary and Poland and the Orthodox state of Kievan Rus'. Kievan Rus' exerted its power through the prosperous kingdom of Galicia, but when that monarchy ceased to exist in the 14th century, Carpathian Rus' remained

A silver belt-end, found in eastern Czechoslovakia and dating from the 9th century. Its design is believed to include pagan as well as Christian iconography.

divided between two states. For the next 500 years, Rusyns living north of the mountains were ruled by the Polish-Lithuanian Commonwealth, those living south of the mountains by the kingdom of Hungary.

The Coming of the Apostles

As it was for many of the other peoples of Europe, the most important event for Carpatho-Rusyns during the early medieval period was their conversion to Christianity. In the 860s, two Byzantine Greek missionaries, the brothers Cyril and Methodius, brought Christianity's teachings northward. They reached the Czechs and Slovaks in the state called Greater Moravia, an area that today includes much of central Czechoslovakia and western Hungary. From there the followers of the Byzantine missionaries brought Christianity and

The brothers Cyril and Methodius—"The Apostles to the Slavs"— brought Christianity to central Europe in the 860s from Constantinople, eastern seat of the church. Legend has it that they established a diocese at Mukachevo, a town in Carpathian Rus'. Rusyn Americans have named many of their churches after them.

the new Slavonic alphabet they had devised eastward to the Carpatho-Rusyns.

This mission of Cyril and Methodius was to become an important milestone in the Carpatho-Rusyn historical tradition. Ever since, local writers have told how the first church diocese in Carpathian Rus', located in the city of Mukachevo, was supposedly one of the seven original dioceses established by Cyril and Methodius; and that another diocese, in nearby Przemyśl, north of the Carpathians, was set up by their followers. Paying tribute to the apostles' work, Rusyn Americans have named many of their churches for Saints Cyril and Methodius.

Another legend tells of the last of the independent rulers of Carpathian Rus', a certain Prince Laborets'. When fierce Magyar tribes from the steppes to the east crossed the Carpathian Mountains and settled in the Danube River basin, fighting ensued. The prince met his death in battle in 899, and eventually the Magyars established the state of Hungary. The coming of the Magyars helped to eliminate the Byzantine Orthodox religious tradition in this part of central Europe, except among the Carpatho-Rusyns.

While their Slovak, Magyar, and Polish neighbors became Western-oriented Roman Catholics, the Carpatho-Rusyns managed to retain their links with the Orthodox East. They did so either directly with the Byzantine Empire or indirectly through the neighboring Kievan Rus' principality and later the kingdom of Galicia. The people's preference for the tradition of the East endured even after Hungary established political control over Carpathian Rus' south of the mountains in the 11th century and after Poland did the same in the north in the 14th century.

Meanwhile, East Slavs from other parts of Galicia continued to settle on the northern and southern slopes of the Carpathians between the 13th and 16th centuries, and they often brought with them Orthodox priests and religious texts. The most important of these newcomers from the east was Prince Fedir Koriatovych. In the late 14th century the Hungarian king granted Koriatovych the castle of Mukachevo, near

The Church of St. Nicholas, at Serednje Vodjane, built in the 17th century in what is now Soviet Transcarpathia. Church architecture in the region, like the people's religion itself, embodies a combination of Eastern and Western influences. A characteristic Carpatho-Rusyn church, like St. Nicholas, makes use of the region's most abundant resource—wood.

An engraving of Prince Fedir Koriatovych, who in the 14th century came to Carpathian Rus' from the east and soon established himself as a political leader. He added to the influence of Orthodox Christianity in the region by establishing a monastery near Mukachevo.

which he established the Monastery of St. Nicholas. For several centuries this monastery was the most important Carpatho-Rusyn cultural center.

Although they lacked political independence, the shepherds and peasant farmers of Carpathian Rus' could be distinguished from their neighbors in two ways. First, they still spoke their East Slavic dialects of old. Second, and more important, they persisted in their adherence to Eastern Christianity. The faith became popularly known as the *rus'ka vira*, or "Rus' faith." So it was that their language, and most especially their faith, came to stand as the primary elements of the Carpatho-Rusyns' distinct ethnic identity.

An important change occurred in the late 16th and 17th centuries. By then, the Carpatho-Rusyns in Poland and Hungary had been reduced to the status of serfs. Serfs were legally bound to the land and subject to the whims of their landlords. Almost all the landlords were of Polish or Hungarian nationality; a few were Austrian. The Carpatho-Rusyns did not accept their new status willingly, and in response several bandits, not unlike Robin Hood, took matters into their hands by robbing estates and distributing the spoils to the poor. The Robin Hood tradition became an important element in local folklore as well as in real life. Carpathian legends celebrate several historic bandits from the 17th and 18th centuries, particularly Oleksa Dovbush, whose exploits made him the most famous of all. In fact, Carpathian bandits were active as recently as the 1920s and 1930s, the best known of these being Mykola Shuhai, who was immortalized soon after his death in a popular Czech novel by Ivan Olbracht, *The Bandit Mykola Shuhai* (*Nikola Šuhaj loupežník*).

But bandit activity never really had a significant or lasting impact on the political situation in Carpathian Rus', where Orthodox priests and bishops remained the only effective Carpatho-Rusyn leaders. Their leadership meant even more after the local churches were cut off in 1453 from the Byzantine center of Orthodoxy in Constantinople following the Turkish conquest of that city. Increasingly, the Carpatho-Rusyns and their priests found themselves isolated among Roman Catholic Polish or Hungarian religious and political officials.

A Religious Compromise

In an attempt to improve their situation, several Orthodox bishops and priests, first in Poland in 1596 and then in Hungary in 1646, pledged their allegiance to the Catholic church in Rome. As part of the contractual agreements known as the Union of Brest (1596) and the Union of Uzhgorod (1646), a new body, called the Uniate church, was created. Although the Uniate church recognized the spiritual and temporal primacy of the pope, it was allowed to retain several of its distinct traditions: It used Church Slavonic instead of Latin for the liturgy; its clergymen were allowed to marry; and it kept the Julian, or "old," calendar. Somewhat later, in 1772, the term *Uniate* was replaced by the name *Greek Catholic*, meaning a Catholic of the Greek, or Byzantine, rite.

With the creation of the Uniate/Greek Catholic Church, the status of the only element in the Carpatho-Rusyn population that could be considered the upper class—the clergy—improved markedly. The clergy was now educated in the best Catholic seminaries in the Hungarian kingdom and later in Austria and Rome. By the end of the 18th century, they had begun to share their knowledge with fellow Carpatho-Rusyns through the establishment of Greek Catholic elementary schools. It was also then that most of the area's wooden churches, the jewels of Carpatho-Rusyn culture, were constructed. They were built by local architects and embellished inside with painted icons— religious images often of Jesus, Mary, or the saints—in a style that developed in the Carpathians from the 9th century onward. These churches and their interiors remain one of the outstanding contributions of Carpatho-Rusyns to European culture.

National Awakening

As in so much of Europe, a new political climate took hold in Carpathian Rus' in the 18th century. By 1711 the Hungarian kingdom, which ruled Carpathian Rus' south of the mountains, had come entirely under Austrian rule. When Poland, which governed the northern part of Carpathian Rus', was absorbed by neighboring powers between 1772 and 1795, its Carpatho-Rusyn lands were incorporated into the new Austrian province of Galicia. All Carpatho-Rusyns now lived within the borders of the Austrian Empire.

Ruled by the House of Hapsburg, the Austrian Empire remained the second largest political entity in Europe (after the Russian Empire) until the end of World War I in 1918. A great collection of nationalities lived within it's borders, and its capital, Vienna, was for many years one of the world's most culturally renowned cities. To get an idea of its size, the empire, known after 1867 as the dual monarchy of Austria-

Aleksander Dukhnovych, the 19th-century poet and cultural leader, is remembered as the "National Awakener of the Carpatho-Rusyns." This monument, unveiled in 1933, still stands in Prešov, the Carpatho-Rusyn cultural center in Czechoslovakia.

Hungary, comprised territory that today includes all of Austria, Hungary, and Czechoslovakia, as well as large parts of Poland, Yugoslavia, Romania, and a chunk of the Soviet Union.

Under Austro-Hungarian rule, there were some cultural advances in Carpathian Rus', including the introduction of compulsory elementary education. The 19th century was also notable as a period of national awakening among Austria-Hungary's many ethnic

The political activist Adolf Dobriansky spoke out on behalf of the Carpatho-Rusyns during the revolution that rocked Austria-Hungary in 1848–49. He served as head of the Rusyn district until it was abolished in early 1850, and later he represented Carpatho-Rusyns in the Hungarian parliament.

groups. Serbs, Croatians, Czechs, Poles, and others all took a renewed pride in their cultural heritage and agitated for political self-determination. In general, these national movements were led by a relatively small, educated segment of society, known as the intelligentsia, who wrote histories of their people, codified and taught their languages, collected their folklore, and wrote, published, and distributed political literature. All this was done in the hope of instilling a sense of pride and political awareness among people who belonged to a distinct nationality, even if the group constituted a minority in a large empire and lacked political independence.

This nationalist revival did not bypass Carpathian Rus', where it was led primarily by two men, Adolf Dobriansky (1817–1901) and Aleksander Dukhnovych (1802–65). Dobriansky was a member of the Hungarian parliament. When Hungarian revolutionaries rebelled against the Austrian government in 1848, he represented Carpatho-Rusyn political and cultural interests before the central government. One year later, after combined Russian and Austrian forces crushed the military of the revolutionary Hungarian republic, Austria resumed absolute control over Hungary. When Hungary's administrative structure was overhauled, Dobriansky became head of the Rusyn district, where he began to implement his policies for national autonomy. Although the Rusyn district was abolished the following year, its brief existence revealed the desire of Carpatho-Rusyns to assert their cultural identity and exercise their political rights.

The work of the other leader, Aleksander Dukhnovych, was purely cultural and perhaps of even greater import. Dukhnovych published the first grammar books written in the Carpatho-Rusyn vernacular, edited the first literary almanacs published in Carpatho-Rusyn, and wrote the text for what became the most famous poem—later the national anthem—of the Carpatho-Rusyns: "I Was, Am and Will Remain a Rusyn" ("Ia Rusyn byl, iesm i budu"). This song is still popular at Carpatho-Rusyn gatherings in the United States. In the European homeland, however, it has been banned by the Communist authorities that have governed Carpathian Rus' since World War II. For the numerous services he performed for his people, Dukhnovych is still remembered as the "national awakener of the Carpatho-Rusyns." After his death, the Carpatho-Rusyn national revival continued through the late 1860s and into the 1870s with the establishment of the first newspapers and cultural organizations and the first efforts to standardize a distinct literary language.

Poverty's Legacy

The 19th century was a period of cultural achievement for the Carpatho-Rusyns, but their economic status worsened during those years. Although serfdom was abolished in 1848, land ownership remained concen-

Carpatho-Rusyn shepherds toting sheep's milk on a farm in the province of Transcarpathia, in the Soviet Ukraine, in 1948. The hilly pastures of Carpathian Rus' have long provided its people with a steady livelihood, but the area's lack of industrial development has meant a relatively low standard of living.

trated in the hands of Hungarian and Austrian aristocrats. Even in the best of times, the peasants found it difficult to survive on their small plots of unproductive mountainous land. By the last decades of the 19th century the situation had become grave. The population continued to grow, and its basic needs could not be provided for on landholdings, often minuscule to begin with, that each family divided among its sons into ever-smaller parcels of land. There was no industry in Carpathian Rus' or in other parts of the underdeveloped Hungarian kingdom and the Austrian province of Galicia, so the factory and manufacturing jobs available to peasants in the areas of Europe that had been transformed by the Industrial Revolution were nonexistent.

As a result, Carpatho-Rusyns sank deeper into poverty, with no hope of improving their situation except by emigrating abroad. Word of the riches to be had in America had begun to filter into southern and eastern Europe by the 1880s, and the glowing reports of readily available land and employment found a receptive audience among Carpatho-Rusyns. Before long, the flow of poverty-stricken peasants in search of economic improvement started westward across the Atlantic to the United States.

With each year the number of Carpatho-Rusyns migrating to America increased. The flow reached its peak during the first decade of the 20th century. By 1914, an estimated 150,000 Carpatho-Rusyns had emigrated to America, and there was hardly a family in the homeland that did not have at least one member in the New World.

In War's Shadow

With the outbreak of World War I in 1914, emigration from eastern and central Europe to the United States practically stopped. The end of the war four years later brought further calamitous changes to the former empires. The Russian Empire was overthrown by revolution in 1917. Austria-Hungary collapsed in October 1918, and the Carpatho-Rusyns, like other minorities once under Hapsburg rule, were forced to decide their

political fate. In late 1918 and early 1919, local leaders organized public meetings at which national councils were formed to discuss and vote on the various political choices open to them. Some called for independence; others wished to remain connected to Hungary or to unite with the Ukraine, with Russia, or with the new state of Czechoslovakia. Carpatho-Rusyns living in what had been Hungary (south of the mountains) decided to join Czechoslovakia; as a precondition, they demanded political and cultural autonomy. They were helped in making this choice by the activity of their immigrant relatives in the United States, who lobbied among the leading Western powers for acceptance of the Czechoslovak solution.

Carpatho-Rusyns living in Galicia (north of the mountains) had fewer choices. Some of them wished to join the West Ukrainian Republic that came into being in late 1918 in the eastern part of Galicia, but most rejected that option. In fact, they even began to distinguish themselves from the Ukrainians in East

As a regiment of lancers from the Austrian imperial army passes through the Lemko Region during World War I, Carpatho-Rusyn peasants point them toward battle against the czarist Russian cavalry. The Austro-Hungarian Empire collapsed at war's end, and this part of historic Carpathian Rus' was absorbed by Poland.

Galicia, who had also called themselves Rusyns. These Carpatho-Rusyns set themselves apart from ethnic Ukrainians with a local name for themselves—Lemko. The Lemko Rusyns wished to unite with their fellow Carpatho-Rusyns south of the mountains in the land they all knew as Carpathian Rus', which meant becoming part of the new state of Czechoslovakia.

Within Czechoslovakia, however, ethnic divisions were already threatening to undermine the fledgling republic, and the Czech government did not wish to add another potentially divisive influence by absorbing the Lemkos' territory. Such an action might also have caused difficulty with the reemergent state of Poland, with which Czechoslovakia hoped to maintain good relations. The Lemkos were rebuffed; in response they decided to establish an independent republic of their own. It lasted only 16 months, until March 1920, by which time Poland had forcibly incorporated all of Galicia, including the Lemko Republic, into its borders.

Carpatho-Rusyns again found themselves in two new states. The majority, about 460,000 people, lived in Czechoslovakia, most of them in the autonomous province of Subcarpathian Rus' (in Czech, Podkarpatská Rus). The remainder, about 200,000 Lemkos living north of the mountains, were governed by Poland. This geographic split was to last until the eve of World War II.

From Self-Rule to Subjugation

During the nearly two decades between the two world wars, Carpatho-Rusyns in Czechoslovakia improved their situation substantially. The government did not grant them the full range of political autonomy it had promised, but the homeland of Subcarpathian Rus' was nonetheless recognized by international treaty and by the Czechoslovak constitution as a distinct territory. (The original proposed name for the independent province was Uhro-Rusinia, a slavicized term for Hungarian Rusyns.) It had its own governor, a partially elected provincial assembly, and a national anthem.

Still more important was the cultural renaissance that began to take root. Carpatho-Rusyns developed their own schools, cultural organizations, theaters, and literature. There also sprang up a distinct school of Subcarpathian painting, whose artists combined the most modern art forms with local Carpatho-Rusyn folk motifs. The cultural revival also stimulated discussion about whether Carpatho-Rusyns were a separate Slavic nationality or whether they were part of the Russian or the Ukrainian nationality.

The Lemko Rusyns in Poland had fewer political and cultural opportunities. They had no self-governing institutions, although in the 1930s they began to establish their own schools, where lessons were taught in the local Lemko Rusyn dialect. In addition, they had their own Uniate Catholic church, a separate apostolic administration created in 1935 by the Vatican as an entity distinct from the Ukrainian church in East Galicia.

These photographs of two Carpatho-Rusyn women in traditional dress were taken in 1920. The cultural renaissance that flourished in Subcarpathian Rus' under Czechoslovakian rule after World War I brought advances in education and contributed to a gradual shift away from historic ways of life.

The shadow of the coming world war signaled an end to self-rule for many peoples. After Germany's Nazi dictator, Adolf Hitler, forced Czechoslovakia to sign the Munich Pact in September 1938, the country was transformed into a federal republic, wherein Czechs, Slovaks, and Carpatho-Rusyns were to rule themselves. (Nazi Germany annexed the regions in which German residents were in the majority.) Subcarpathian Rus' finally received full political autonomy, and by the end of the year those local leaders who identified themselves as Ukrainians, led by Msgr. Avhustyn Voloshyn, came to dominate the province and renamed it Carpatho-Ukraine. On March 15, 1939, they declared the Carpatho-Ukraine an independent state.

Independence was extremely short-lived. That very same day, March 15, Hitler's Germany, in cooperation with its allies, decided to eliminate Czechoslovakia from the map of Europe. The Carpatho-Rusyns of Czechoslovakia found themselves once again under Hungarian rule, with about 80,000 of them left in the northeast corner of a pro-German Slovak state. A few months later, in September, Hitler turned his attention and his armies to Poland. After obtaining the Soviet Union's guarantee that it would not interfere, Hitler liquidated that country as well, and the Lemko Rusyns living there fell under German rule.

Hungarian and German rule over Carpathian Rus' lasted until the final months of World War II. In late 1944 the Soviet Red Army entered the region, and by the spring of 1945 new borders were drawn.

Under Three Masters

The Carpatho-Rusyns found themselves divided among three new states, a situation that prevails today. South of the mountains, Subcarpathian Rus' (occupied during the war by Hungary) became part of the Soviet Union and was renamed the Transcarpathian Oblast of the Ukrainian Soviet Socialist Republic. It measures about 5,000 square miles, slightly larger than the state of Connecticut. (An *oblast* is a Soviet administrative unit comparable to a province.) The Soviet Union argued that the local Slavic population, by then about 550,000 people, were ethnic Ukrainians and wished to join their brethren to the east. Another 100,000 Carpatho-Rusyns were left in the northeast corner of Czechoslovakia, in the Prešov region of Slovakia.

North of the mountains, the Lemko Rusyns came under the rule of a restored Poland, but their situation was worse than that of their compatriots south of the mountains. As a result of agreements between the Soviet Union and Poland on the transfer of populations, in 1945–46 the 200,000 Lemko Rusyns were told they had to leave their homes. At first, about two-thirds of them were resettled to the east, in the Soviet Ukraine (but not with their ethnic kin in the Transcarpathian Oblast). When the remaining one-third refused to leave, they were forcibly deported in 1947 to the western and northern regions of Poland, on lands acquired by that country from defeated Germany after the war.

Central Europe today. The shaded areas are the lands inhabited by Carpatho-Rusyn people in present-day Czechoslovakia and the Soviet Union. Their ethnic brethren north of the mountains, the Lemkos of Poland, were dispersed by the Communist government after World War II. Some Carpatho-Rusyns also live in Yugoslavia, having emigrated in the 18th century.

Peasants attending class at an agricultural school on a state-run farm in the Transcarpathian Oblast of the Soviet Ukraine, in the late 1940s. Although economic life improved somewhat under Soviet rule, the Carpatho-Rusyns were officially classified as Ukrainians, and their political liberties were restricted.

Under postwar Polish law, these 70,000 Lemko Rusyns were forbidden to return to the ancestral Carpathian homeland, although since the 1960s about 10,000 people have managed, with great difficulty, to do so.

Still Between Two Worlds

The new political environment has brought about profound change throughout Carpathian Rus'. By 1948, all three countries ruling the area had established Communist governments, with Poland and Czechoslovakia functioning as satellites of the Soviet Union. Besides the one-party political system established by these governments, Communist rule has also meant the end of private enterprise (individually owned shops, small businesses, and factories) in all three countries. Private landholding is allowed only in Poland, so most Carpatho-Rusyn farmers now work for local state-run farms. The new economic system has brought an end to the relative poverty once common in most villages, and today Carpatho-Rusyns lead an economically secure existence. They gain their livelihood either from the land or by traveling to nearby towns and cities to work in the new factories that have been built in the postwar years.

Under communism, the previously dominant role of religion in Carpatho-Rusyn life was lessened. The Greek Catholic church was outlawed between 1946 and 1950, with its members forcibly transformed into adherents of Orthodoxy or, as was more often the case, urged by officially atheistic governments to cease their Christian practices altogether. Only in Czechoslovakia was the Greek Catholic church legally restored. Since 1968 it has carried on side by side with Orthodoxy in Carpatho-Rusyn villages in the Prešov region.

At the same time that these changes in religious life were being enforced, the people were also compelled to abandon their ethnic name. The older names—Rusyn, Rusnak, Lemko—were no longer recognized; Soviet, Czechoslovak, and Polish officials declared everyone in the group to be Ukrainian. Some persons welcomed the change, some did not. For instance, in Czechoslovakia and Poland, tens of thousands of Carpatho-Rusyns registered their protest individually by calling themselves Slovak or Polish rather than Ukrainian.

Between 1945 and the late 1960s, the Soviet, Czechoslovak, and Polish governments placed stringent restrictions on travel to and from Carpathian Rus', which is considered militarily sensitive because of its location near so many international borders. The restrictions added to the feeling of physical and psychological separation between Carpatho-Rusyn Americans and their relatives in Europe. With the European group's political liberty diminished, its religious activity officially limited, and its very name—Rusyn, Rusnak, Lemko—either legislated out of existence or rendered devoid of meaning, the Carpatho-Rusyns' sense of identity suffered.

Three trembita players in Soviet Transcarpathia. The musical instrument, unique to this region, is made of pine and birch wood. Ethnic pride among Carpatho-Rusyns has surged since the 1960s, resulting in a renewed interest in their traditional culture.

However, with the political changes in Eastern Europe during the 1980s, there has been a return to certain traditional values. In Poland, some Lemko Rusyns are petitioning the authorities to recognize them as a group distinct from Poles and Ukrainians. In Soviet Transcarpathia, the Carpatho-Rusyns have been proudly proclaiming their regional pride and patriotism for years, as a way of setting themselves off from the rest of the Ukraine. Some people in the region have been active since the 1970s in a movement that presses the government to restore the Greek Catholic church to legal status. And late in the 1980s, the Communist governments began to allow a small increase in the number of privately owned farms and enterprises, although not everyone has benefited from this shift in policy.

Since World War II, Carpatho-Rusyns have been able to find a life free of repression only in Yugoslavia and North America. In the former, a group of about 25,000 Carpatho-Rusyns (whose ancestors had immigrated there in the 18th century) are recognized as a distinct national minority, one with its own literary language, that is used in government-supported schools and publications. And in the United States and Canada, the descendants of Carpatho-Rusyn immigrants, despite what has transpired in the homeland since their ancestors left before World War I, continue to preserve a distinct Carpatho-Rusyn identity and community life.

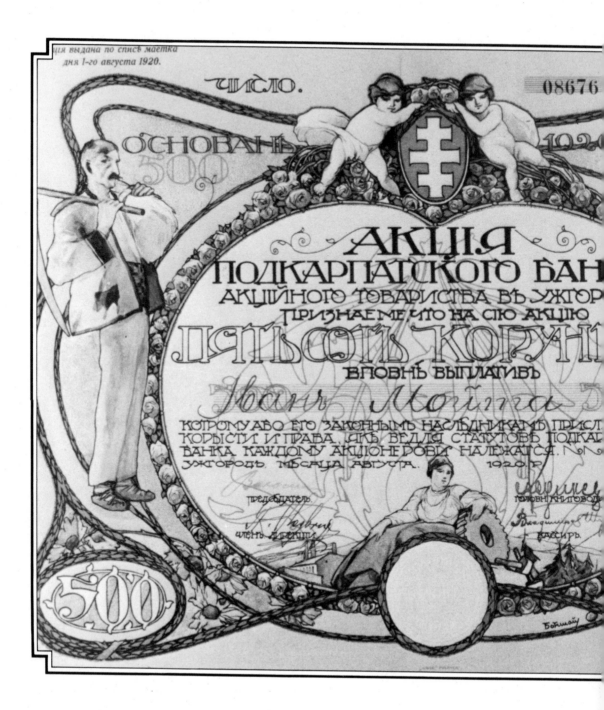

EVENTS OF THE IMMIGRATION

Because many different foreign powers have
ruled Carpathian Rus' in the distant and recent past, the first immigrants and their
descendants often did not identify themselves as Carpatho-Rusyns. For this reason, shipping records and
U.S. statistical reports often are misleading. The vast
majority of Carpatho-Rusyn immigrants left Europe
between 1880 and 1918, when Carpathian Rus' was still
part of the Austro-Hungarian Empire. To this day,
many old-timers will remember fondly and even
proudly that they or their parents were born in Austria
as subjects of the popular Hapsburg emperor Francis
Joseph I, who reigned from 1848 to 1916. Others who
left later, when the empire had been supplanted by
Czechoslovakia or Poland, tend to link their background with those countries.

Even if Carpatho-Rusyn Americans are well aware
that they are not Austrians or Hungarians or Czechs
or Slovaks or Poles, they usually find it easier to identify themselves to fellow Americans by reference to a
known country—Austria, Hungary, Czechoslovakia,

The citizens of Danylove gather at the town well in 1921. The majority of Carpatho-Rusyns knew little about life outside their town or village and were unprepared for the fast pace of life in America.

or Poland—than to explain the complex problem of what it means to belong to a national minority in a multinational region or state. Other national minorities are often misidentified in a similar fashion. For example, the Welsh are sometimes described as English or the Catalans as Spanish.

So it is that official statistical data can do little in helping to uncover precisely how many Carpatho-Rusyns came to the United States. At best, the historian and student can rely only on indirect evidence and estimates, which suggest that between 125,000 and 150,000 Carpatho-Rusyns arrived before 1914. These figures are based on an analysis of the membership rolls of the group's churches and political and fraternal organizations. Although less reliable than statistical data, oral history—the spoken reminiscences of the immigrant generation and their descendants about how many of their family and friends made the trek to the New World—also supports these estimates.

The greatest hindrance to further immigration was the outbreak of World War I, which effectively blocked most transatlantic movement until about 1920. But by then, some factions in American society were concerned about the large number of recent immigrants who were not from northern or western Europe. So the U.S. government began to restrict immigration from southern and eastern Europe, and in 1924 it established quotas that strictly limited the number of people from those areas who could enter the country.

In about 1900, a Slavic woman at the immigration center at Ellis Island, in New York harbor, takes a test to detect mental retardation. Immigrants had to undergo a battery of medical tests and provide satisfactory answers to a series of questions before they were allowed to enter the United States.

As a result, only about 7,500 Carpatho-Rusyns came to America during the 1920s. With the United States basically closed, other countries, especially Canada, seemed more promising: About 10,000 Carpatho-Rusyns, in particular Lemkos from Poland, went to Canada during the late 1920s and 1930s. Whereas the United States has been more lenient in its policies toward newcomers since World War II, restrictions in the Communist-ruled European homeland have not been eased. Those governments have permitted only a few hundred Carpatho-Rusyns to depart in recent years. Emigration has occurred during periods of political crises, such as Czechoslovakia's Prague Spring of 1968–69 (a popular movement bent on loosening state control, crushed by Soviet troops) and the height of the Solidarity movement in Poland in the early 1980s, when industrial workers organized to demand liberalizing reforms.

Today there are an estimated 690,000 Americans who have come from Carpathian Rus' or who can claim at least one Carpatho-Rusyn ancestor. The number in Canada, following subsequent immigration to the United States, is much smaller—only about 10,000 people.

Getting There

Like the other eastern and southern Europeans who streamed to America in the decades just before World War I, Carpatho-Rusyns crossed the Atlantic Ocean on ships that were often overcrowded and unsanitary. Disease thrived under these conditions; death at sea was not uncommon. Upon arriving in New York harbor, in the shadow of the Statue of Liberty, the newcomers were ferried along the New Jersey side of the harbor to Ellis Island, site of the U.S. government's main immigration processing center. Having left behind family, friends, and homeland, the eager and often frightened new arrivals were asked to wait in the great hall of the main building. They then underwent a medical examination, a procedure many had never before experienced, and were asked to answer a number of questions concerning their medical history, des-

Immigrant children and their guardians at Ellis Island, about 1905. Several thousand Carpatho-Rusyns arrived in America each year in the three decades before World War I. Typically, a father would emigrate first, then send money to pay for his family's passage.

tination in the United States, and other matters. The thought that a wrong answer or a hacking cough might be enough to allow an immigration official to turn them away made many immigrants nervous. Still, the vast majority were allowed to enter. The newcomers could then get their papers stamped and be off to their first home in the New World. For those whose medical condition did not meet a certain standard—if the immigrant was thought to be carrying a communicable disease, for example—the wait could be extended for several days. Those whose papers were not in order might also be detained. Some were even sent back to Europe by the U.S. authorities, a fate that befell thousands of European immigrants, though comparatively few Carpatho-Rusyns.

Top: *A Carpatho-Rusyn family's hut in the homeland, before World War I.* Bottom: *Housing for immigrant workers outside of Lattimer, Pennsylvania, 1898. The shock of leaving the Old World for the New World could be great, and few who made the trip knew what they would find.*

Although this is a fair description of the characteristic experience of the early Carpatho-Rusyn immigrants, it does not fully convey what it meant to leave one's loved ones to embark on a long and often arduous journey or what it meant to feel that at the end of the trip there still loomed the great unknown. For that experience, the tales of individual immigrants can paint a vivid picture.

One day in 1914, [writes her granddaughter, Patricia Krafcik] sixteen-year-old Anna Bujdosh embraced her mother warmly and kissed her tear-stained cheeks and lips. Then, clutching a small bundle of belongings and food, she took her place on the back of an open horse-drawn cart and let her legs swing down over the side in rhythm with the cart's rocking movement. Tears stung her eyes as the cart pulled away from her village, Ruská Vol'a. She gave a last long look at the humble wood and white-washed house, the rolling mountains in the distance, and at her mother waving and calling out, "Come back soon!" Come back soon—but in her mother's strong face, Anna read a different message: If my life has been hard, God grant that you make yours better. Live now not for me, live for yourself, your children, and your grandchildren.

At this moment of departure, however, Anna needed the comfort of knowing that she would return. After a long journey across an ocean, she would meet her own people in New York and New Jersey (these were still only strange place-names to her), find work, and then take her income back home to help her family. All this at sixteen years of age? To me now, her granddaughter, this seems inconceivable, but it seemed perfectly possible to Anna and to thousands of young Carpatho-Rusyn men and women like her.

For another Carpatho-Rusyn, getting to North America was more dangerous, at least as the saga was retold by a grandson. But the result was the same: a successful arrival.

Paul Lengyel had just finished building a roof for a new house in his native Carpathian mountain village in northeastern Hungary. His two-year-old daughter was healthy, and his wife was carrying another child. Things seemed to be going so well. Even if he was in debt for the house, he felt confident about being able to pay it off. But this was the spring of 1914, and Lengyel soon received official notice that he would be drafted into the Austro-Hungarian Imperial Army. This news could not have come at a worse time. How was

Carpatho-Rusyn children praying at a shrine in the homeland village of Iasynia, circa 1920. Their religion was perhaps the most important aspect of their culture that the Carpatho-Rusyns brought with them to America.

he to pay off his mortgage? How was he to support his young, growing family?

There was only one answer to his dilemma. Like his older relatives and friends had done before, he would go work in America to make enough money to set things straight at home. Lengyel was joined by seven other young men who began the several-hundred-mile walk south through Transylvania across the arc of the Carpathian Mountain range into Romania. The group was forced to travel at night, since Hungarian police were rounding up all able-bodied men for service in the army. Finally, they reached the Black Sea port of Constantsa [in Romania], and from there they boarded a ship to Greece and then to America.

Like Anna and Paul, most Carpatho-Rusyns who left the homeland before World War I were intent on returning home just as soon as they could earn extra money. Whereas in the decades before 1914 many of the immigrants did cross and recross the Atlantic several times, the war put an end to that; the vast majority of those who came to North America never went back. If they wished to be reminded of their homeland, they had to recreate part of it in the New World.

Steelworkers in Pennsylvania in the 1890s. Carpatho-Rusyn immigrants were among those who filled the need for manual laborers created by America's Industrial Revolution.

THE NEW WORLD

Most Carpatho-Rusyn immigrants made their first home relatively close to their arrival point, the port of New York. There were two reasons for their decision to settle in that part of the country: The industrial Northeast had jobs that needed to be filled, and the newcomers needed to find work fast and earn money. Most Carpatho-Rusyns were not planning to stay in America; they intended to earn money quickly so they could return home as soon as possible, where with their new wealth they hoped to get out of debt and buy more land. This desire corresponded nicely with the increasing need of American industrialists for manpower. Between 1865 (the end of the Civil War) and 1914 (the beginning of World War I), the United States completed its transition from a predominantly agricultural to an industrial nation. During that period, the United States made the transformation from a nation built of wood and stone to one built of iron, steel, and concrete. Technological advances and the discovery of huge mineral deposits made possible America's Industrial Revolution; immigrant labor provided the sweat that kept the mines, mills, and refineries going. Once their processing at Ellis Island was completed, Carpatho-Rusyns moved quickly to the new mining and industrial sites.

They went first, in the 1880s and 1890s, to the anthracite coalfields of eastern Pennsylvania. By the turn of the 20th century, they had begun to move farther west to the steel mills of Pittsburgh and its suburbs.

Andrew Julo, an immigrant coal miner in Pennsylvania, was identified as a Ruthenian, a term under which Carpatho-Rusyns were often labeled in the New World. In the mining and industrial towns and valleys where most Eastern European immigrants settled, ethnic and class solidarity was often tested by each individual's desire to make a good life for him- or herself.

Before long, the greater Pittsburgh area became the unofficial capital of the Carpatho-Rusyn people in America. The New York City metropolitan area, especially north-central and northeastern New Jersey, with its various manufacturing and oil-refining plants, was the second most popular location for Carpatho-Rusyns in search of work.

By 1920, the Carpatho-Rusyn settlement pattern was more or less fixed. The urban areas of the Middle Atlantic states, especially in Pennsylvania (54 percent), New York (13 percent), and New Jersey (12 percent), accounted for 79 percent of all Carpatho-Rusyns in the United States. The group also settled in large concentrations in Connecticut, Ohio, and Illinois. Some even ventured to places farther away, where relatively high paying mine jobs were available, such as Vermont, Minnesota, Oklahoma, Montana, and Washington. For Carpatho-Rusyn immigrants, the lure of the frontier was explained as much by the presence of jobs as by the desire for the wide open spaces or the spirit of adventure. Working the western mines also afforded the newcomers from Carpathian Rus' the opportunity to live in a small mountain town similar (at least in size) to the homeland village.

The concentration of Carpatho-Rusyns and their American-born descendants in the Northeast has not changed substantially to this day. Most of the group's churches and secular organizations are still found there. Only during the last two decades have some of the older or more economically mobile individuals followed the lead of many other Americans and moved toward the Sun Belt, in particular to Florida in the Southeast and to California in the West.

That a significant Carpatho-Rusyn community still lives in the United States, let alone that it is spread out across the continent, is somewhat ironic, because most of the immigrants who arrived between 1880 and 1914 never dreamed that they and their descendants would remain in America permanently. Almost four-fifths of the newcomers were males who had left their families in Europe. They had come to work for a few years in order to save as many dollars as possible and then

return home, with any luck to join the small ranks of the village rich. In chasing that dream, the Carpatho-Rusyns exchanged their European way of life as small-scale farmers and shepherds in the verdant Carpathian Mountains for long hours of backbreaking work in the coal mines of eastern Pennsylvania, the steel mills of the greater Pittsburgh area, or as unskilled and semi-skilled laborers in the mills and factories of New York, New Jersey, Connecticut, Ohio, Indiana, and Illinois.

Settling In

It was not long before some of the younger Carpatho-Rusyn men decided to make America their new, permanent home. With the outbreak of World War I, most others were forced to make the same choice, because the devastating conflict closed off their European homeland to further visits and even to letters. After the war ended in 1918, only a few Carpatho-Rusyns took advantage of the opportunity to return to Europe. The majority had already married and started families in the United States, or else they quickly sent for their wives and children to join them in the New World.

Carpatho-Rusyn immigrants held jobs mainly at the low end of the American economic scale, as coal breakers and haulers, stokers, ditchdiggers, or machine operators. As such, they were hardly held in

The "Street of Rocks" in Shenandoah, Pennsylvania, in the 1890s. This grimy mining town was one of the first in which Carpatho-Rusyns built their own parish church. Considering the poverty in which many of them lived, it is remarkable that Carpatho-Rusyn immigrants were able to devote so much time, energy, and money to establish their religion in the New World.

high regard by native-born Americans or by other immigrants who had arrived before them. Lumped together with other Slavs and Hungarians, the Carpatho-Rusyns were often called "Hunkies." Yet such discrimination could be overcome, as there was usually an opportunity to work. For the practical-minded Carpatho-Rusyn worker, worrying about the lack of respect took a backseat to acquiring "the almighty dollar" as the key to success in America.

The few Carpatho-Rusyn women who came to America at this time also played an active role during these early years of immigration. Economic necessity oftentimes forced them to be liberated from the household in a manner that few of them desired. Women earned income from part-time or full-time work as store clerks or mill hands, as maids or servants in the homes of wealthy persons, or as operators of boardinghouses in their own homes. Of course, added to these responsibilities were the usual household chores, unavoidable in that era, of cooking, cleaning, and taking care of the children.

Those Carpatho-Rusyn immigrants who were not able or not allowed to work in the factories and mines had to find other ways to supplement the family income. As seen here, women and children sometimes scavenged for coal, wood, and other combustibles to heat their homes.

Over time, Carpatho-Rusyns and their descendants have been able to enter the economic mainstream of middle-class America without undue difficulty. By the 1930s and 1940s, most of the second generation was completing high school and entering the work force as skilled laborers, managers, or foremen. Since the 1950s, college and university education has been common, so that teachers, nurses, and industry managers are well represented today among Americans of Carpatho-Rusyn background.

The Shock of the New

During this process of economic advancement, the traditional Carpatho-Rusyn way of life brought from Europe had to change, sometimes quite radically. The most significant alteration was the switch from working in the daylight and fresh air, tending cows, sheep, and a small plot of land, to laboring in the dark bowels of the Pennsylvania earth or surrounded by the deafening noise of industrial machinery in dreary factories. As part of this change, the comparatively relaxed work cycle in rural parts, determined by the seasons and the daily "sun clock," was replaced by 10- and 12-hour work shifts measured by a mercilessly precise mechanical timepiece.

The American-born Carpatho-Rusyns who began to enter the work force in large numbers during the 1920s and 1930s found the adjustment to industrial life somewhat easier than did their parents. After all, the second generation had grown up in the shadow of the mine, mill, or factory, and urban life in cramped living quarters was the only life many of them knew. Nevertheless, both the immigrants and their American-born children felt the need to retain some of the traditions they brought from the old country. For Carpatho-Rusyns, the most important of these traditions—the very center of their life, on both spiritual and social grounds—was the church.

The close relationship of Carpatho-Rusyns to their church had been sacred in the European homeland until Carpathian Rus' came under Communist rule in the late 1940s. The whole cycle of village life was governed

Assembly-line workers, including many Carpatho-Rusyn women, in a shoe factory in Johnson City, New York, circa 1930. For the children and grandchildren of immigrants, a skilled trade and better standard of living became a possibility.

by the rhythm of the climate and the agricultural seasons, interspersed with an obligatory day of full rest and worship each Sunday. Numerous other feasts connected with the church calendar as well as individual ceremonies relating to birth, marriage, and death also offered respite from the daily toil. For Carpatho-Rusyns, participation in a church-centered function was as natural—and as necessary, both psychologically and culturally—as eating and sleeping.

It is not surprising, therefore, that the first Carpatho-Rusyn immigrants, even those who had come only temporarily, worked hard to re-create the religious environment of the world they had left behind. Even today, a century after the first immigrants arrived, Rusyn-American community life tends to revolve primarily around individual parishes.

Translating the Past

For the most part, Carpatho-Rusyns are Eastern Christians. This means that their form of worship derives from the Orthodox, or Byzantine, tradition. Their services were (and in some cases still are) conducted in Church Slavonic (a liturgical language common to all East Slavs) and sung without organ accompaniment; the priests have the option to marry or to remain celibate; and the church observes the Julian calendar, according to which fixed holidays such as Christmas (January 7th) and New Year (January 14th) fall nearly two weeks later than they would if the Western, or Gregorian, calendar of the Roman Catholic church were used. To the passerby, Eastern Christian churches stand out by virtue of two common features: golden domes and three-barred crosses on the outside, and, on the inside, iconostases (tall screens covered with depictions, called icons, of religious figures), which that separate the altar from the congregation.

These features of Eastern Christianity remained in place in Carpatho-Rusyn houses of worship even after Orthodoxy was replaced by the Uniate church in the course of the 16th and 17th centuries. Consequently, the first Carpatho-Rusyn immigrants who arrived in America during the decades before World War I were in union with the Roman Catholic church but practiced essentially the same rituals as those of the Orthodox church.

It was their fidelity to Eastern practices that got Carpatho-Rusyn Catholics into trouble in America. By the closing decades of the 19th century, Roman Catholics were attempting to create one American Catholic church that would not be divided along ethnic lines or by differences in ritual. American Catholic bishops were unsympathetic, and even hostile, to the Greek Catholic church in America, to which many Carpatho-Rusyns and Ukrainians belonged. The bishops were particularly opposed to such deviations from the Roman church practice as married priests.

Those early years, then, were very difficult for Carpatho-Rusyns. On the one hand, they were trying to survive economically in an industrial environment for which nothing in their largely agricultural past experience had prepared them. On the other hand, they were attempting to preserve their Eastern Christian rites in a Roman Catholic world that was fundamentally opposed to their traditional ways. Nor was the conflict limited to discussions among theologians and religious experts. The people themselves were directly affected, and it was not uncommon for a Carpatho-

Reverend and Mrs. Andrew Ivan and their daughter, Andrea. As practitioners of the Greek (or Byzantine) Catholic rite, Carpatho-Rusyn priests were traditionally allowed to marry, which is not the custom in the Roman Catholic church. In the early decades of the 20th century, this difference led to tensions and divisions within the larger Catholic community in America.

A procession leaves St. Mary's Church in Minneapolis, Minnesota, after a service in 1934. The church was founded in 1887 by Carpatho-Rusyn followers of the Greek Catholic rite; they later converted to Russian Orthodoxy to be free from the strictures imposed by the Roman Catholic hierarchy in America.

Rusyn to be denied the services of a Catholic priest for a baptism, a wedding, or even a burial because he or she persisted in adhering to Eastern Catholic practices.

The immigrants had come too far to be discouraged, however. While some responded by giving up the Eastern rite and joining Roman Catholic churches, mainly those attended by fellow Slavs, especially Poles or Slovaks, most of them simply built their own churches and invited Greek Catholic priests from Europe to come and administer to their spiritual needs. The invitation usually included a promise to pay for the priest's journey. The initiative shown by laymen in these working-class parishes, along with their ambitious priests, led to the establishment of the first Carpatho-Rusyn Catholic churches in eastern Pennsylvania—at Shenandoah in 1884, at Freeland in 1886, at Hazleton in 1887—and even one as far west as Minneapolis, Minnesota, in 1887.

Conflict in the Ranks

As more immigrants arrived and the Greek Catholic community grew, conflict with the Roman Catholic church increased. Some Carpatho-Rusyn priests and parishes reacted to the problem by returning to what they considered the old faith—Orthodoxy. The first parish to make such a move was the Greek Catholic Church of St. Mary in Minneapolis, headed by a Carpatho-Rusyn priest, the Reverend Alexis G. Toth. Convinced that his own action was the correct path, Toth undertook a missionary journey to Carpatho-Rusyn communities in Pennsylvania. His efforts were successful, and by 1914, an estimated 25,000 Carpatho-Rusyns had, as he and others said, "returned to Orthodoxy." They joined the Russian Orthodox church (in the United States it has been called the Orthodox Church in America since 1970), at least half of whose members are still of Carpatho-Rusyn heritage. So it was that by the time the great wave of Carpatho-Rusyn immigration ended in 1914, the Carpatho-Rusyns were divided into the Greek Catholics and the Orthodox.

At about this same time, Carpatho-Rusyns became divided from other Greek Catholics who came from the eastern part of the Austrian province of Galicia, just north of the Carpathian Mountains. The division here was over ethnic identity, but it spread to religious life. Though the Galicians had once called themselves Rusyns, before long they identified themselves in America as Ukrainians, a name that, they argued, underscored their status as a distinct East Slavic nationality.

In Europe, the Carpatho-Rusyns had been divided for centuries by a political border that ran along the crest of the Carpathians. Although Rusyns north and south of the mountains belonged to the same church and spoke similar dialects, after centuries of living under Hungarian and Polish rule people in the two regions had developed different customs, cultural lives,

The iconostasis, or icon screen, of St. Mary's Byzantine Catholic Church, Kingston, Pennsylvania, exemplifies this traditional feature of Eastern Christian churches. Flanked by murals, the screen depicts Christ (top), the Last Supper (middle), the 4 evangelists, the 12 apostles, Mary, and other scenes.

and aspirations. These differences became especially evident when the two groups met on American soil.

The Carpatho-Rusyns wished to retain their unique form of church singing (the *prostopinye*, or plainchant); their own dialects, which were used in publications and were taught in community schools; and most especially the names Rus' and Rusyn, which the Rusyns from East Galicia had dropped in favor of Ukrainian. To validate their religious practices in the New World, the Carpatho-Rusyns also wanted their own Greek Catholic bishop. But when they finally received one, in 1907, they bitterly opposed him because he was a Ukrainian from East Galicia.

One way to oppose the Ukrainian leadership in the American Catholic church was to defect to Orthodoxy, and many Carpatho-Rusyns did just that. The move to Orthodoxy was particularly popular among the Lemkos, who came from the western part of Galicia and like their fellow Carpatho-Rusyns south of the mountains did not wish to identify themselves as Ukrainians.

In the world of Orthodoxy, the Carpatho-Rusyns hoped to have their own bishops and to retain their identity as the people of Rus'. Meanwhile, those Carpatho-Rusyns who did not defect to Orthodoxy continued to demand their own Greek Catholic bishop. Although these controversies were played out in the context of the church, they reflected deeper cultural differences. The Vatican, too, came to realize that the differences between Carpatho-Rusyns and Ukrainians outweighed their similarities, and to avoid further problems it divided them in 1916 into separate Greek Catholic jurisdictions. By 1924, Carpatho-Rusyns and Ukrainians each had received their own bishops, and two distinct churches, each with its own hierarchy, exist to this day.

Thus, by the end of their great wave of immigration, the Carpatho-Rusyns had succeeded in defining and preserving their distinctiveness from other eastern and central European immigrant groups. Hoping to hold on to certain Old World traditions, the immigrants had been able to retain some of their most important cultural practices, including their religious rites. Yet as the years went by, few of the immigrants were unaware that as they sought to preserve what was familiar, they had also begun to adapt to the new environment in which they found themselves.

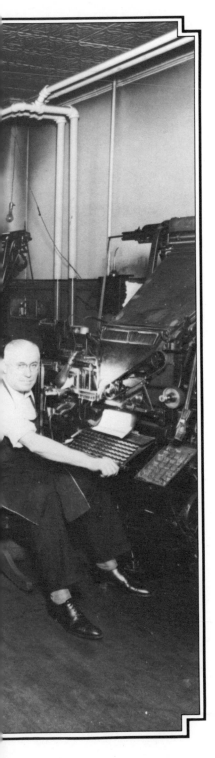

Moving into the skilled professions: the manager and linotypists in the printing department of the Greek Catholic Union (GCU) in Munhall, Pennsylvania, in 1947. Founded in 1892, the GCU is still the largest fraternal organization of Carpatho-Rusyns in the New World.

ASSIMILATION AND ADAPTATION

I n a certain sense, the history of American society is largely the story of economic assimilation and cultural adaptation by the millions of immigrants who came to this continent from elsewhere. For most newcomers, freedom has meant the ability to earn a livelihood in order to support oneself and one's family with dignity. Immigrants were therefore most willing to adopt whatever characteristics they felt were necessary to obtain some degree of financial security. In this regard, Carpatho-Rusyns and their descendants, like most of the other older European immigrant groups who came primarily before World War I, have become completely Americanized.

The process of cultural adaptation has raised a number of questions for both Carpatho-Rusyn individuals and the group as a whole. How many Old World customs and traditions must be given up for the sake of economic advancement? How many of these should be maintained in order to preserve a sense of identity and self-worth? In a number of ways, it is the effort to find an answer to these questions that has determined the history of Carpatho-Rusyns in America.

Perhaps the area in which assimilation has been greatest is language. Although it is true that among unskilled and semiskilled industrial workers it was relatively easy to get along while speaking the native tongue, economic advancement required knowledge of English. In this regard, Carpatho-Rusyn Americans have been active cultural assimilators, even in the Slavic neighborhoods where they first lived in great numbers.

The Language Shift

Loss of the native language did not occur overnight, however, as demonstrated by the vibrant Carpatho-Rusyn-language press that thrived in the United States from the 1890s to the 1940s and in Canada after World

The title page of Niva, *a Rusyn-American literary and religious magazine published briefly in 1916. The first 40 years of the 20th century were the heyday of the group's publishing ventures, with many weekly papers printed in both the United States and Canada. These periodicals did much to unite the many different Carpatho-Rusyn immigrant communities.*

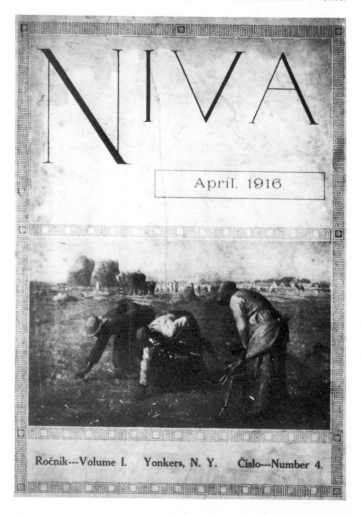

NIVA

April, 1916

Ročnik---Volume I.   Yonkers, N. Y.   Čislo---Number 4.

War I. The press included several weeklies, monthlies, and even one daily newspaper, *Den'* (the *Day*), which appeared from 1922 to 1926. These papers also encouraged literary endeavor, as evidenced by the presence in their pages of many original poems and short stories written by Carpatho-Rusyn Americans. One short-lived journal, *Niva* (*The Sown Field*), which ran for 11 monthly issues in 1916, was devoted exclusively to Carpatho-Rusyn literature. And one author, Emilij Kubek, published several poems about the life of immigrants and a popular novel about life in the European homeland.

In one poem, "Ci lem viditsja mi?" ("Does It Only Seem So to Me?"), Kubek examined a dilemma faced by many of the early immigrants: Can happiness ever be found in America, or are the beauties of life to be had only in the Carpathian homeland?

> My thoughts even now fall
>   on the Carpathians,
> On my native land that
>   I cannot forget.
> Although in my youth
>   fortune did smile on me,
> And I frequently had to struggle
>   from want;
> And although over there in the homeland
> Things were frequently lacking,
> Still now the native land remains
>   always dear.
> I must remember the graves
> In which my children, my father,
>   and my mother lie—
> Would it not be better to
>   lie next to them?
> My thoughts go unto you, oh native land:
> Are the evenings, summers, the land, and
>   the coffins
> More beautiful over there?
> Or does it only seem so,
> Do I only imagine it?

The Carpatho-Rusyn-language press and the various literary efforts were read primarily by the first-generation immigrants who came before World War I. Their children exhibited a lesser interest in reading the language of the homeland. The very format of the newspapers revealed a gradual but steady change. By the early 1920s, the Cyrillic alphabet had been replaced in most publications by the Latin alphabet, and by the late 1940s half of the articles in most newspapers were in English. By the late 1960s, language assimilation was virtually complete, and by the late 1980s there were only two newspapers that still printed half their articles in Carpatho-Rusyn. They were *Karpatska Rus'* (*Carpatho-Rus*), printed in Yonkers, New York, and *Karpatorusskije otzvuki* (*Carpatho-Russian Echoes*), printed in Fort Lauderdale, Florida.

The reasons for these changes were twofold. For one, speaking English was the usual ticket toward greater economic and professional success. For another, many Carpatho-Rusyns in America had a sense of embarrassment and shame about their various spoken dialects, which they thought were somehow uncultured mixtures unworthy of comparison with the better-known Slavic languages (Czech, Polish, Slovak, and Russian), let alone a world language such as English. Certainly not every immigrant felt this way, but those who did were numerous enough to prevail within the community. In the struggle between old and new, assimilation won out and children were urged to use English. Even first-generation parents, when they could, preferred to use broken English rather than the fluent roll of their native speech.

New Churches, New Lives

There was one area, however, in which Carpatho-Rusyn Americans were adamant about preserving and defending their traditional culture. This was religious life. Their means of holding on to their Eastern Christian traditions took different forms. Greek Catholics refused to abide by American Catholic norms; others rejected Catholicism in favor of converting, or "returning," to Orthodoxy. Many converts among this latter

(continued on page 73)

Overleaf: *Rusyn-American parishioners receiving communion at Holy Ghost Orthodox Catholic Church in Phoenixville, Pennsylvania. An ornate icon screen graces the chancel.*

A service (above) during the Christmas season at St. Nicholas Carpatho-Russian Church, on East 10th Street in New York City. Inscribed on the baldachin, the wooden canopy over the altar, are the words Otche Nash—Our Father. Left: A priest blesses egg baskets after the Easter service at the church. Festively painted and adorned Easter eggs are one of the many Old World traditions that Rusyn Americans have preserved.

During a Rusyn-American wedding ceremony (left) in Parma, Ohio, the priest holds a crown above the groom's, then the bride's head, a tradition in Eastern Christian churches that symbolizes the Kingdom of God the couple now enters together. On the Just Married sign (above), Carpatho-Rusyn peasants dance a wedding step.

The Rusyn-American community often gathers over traditional foods, which have made their way onto many an American menu. Pirohi (below), triangular pieces of stuffed pasta, are a popular dish in neighborhood restaurants in the northeastern United States and are a staple at church and social functions. Halushki (noodles) and kolbasi (spiced sausages) are also traditional.

Menu
FILLED CABBAGE
PIROHI
ROAST BEEF SAND.
KOLBASI ᵂ/Kraut
HALUSHKI
CHICKEN SOUP
HOT DOGS
COFFEE
SODA
AKE

Breads, cookies in the shape of a three-barred Eastern Christian cross, and other delectables are offered after the Easter service at St. Nicholas Church in New York.

(continued from page 64)

group struggled within the Russian Orthodox church to create distinct Carpatho-Rusyn dioceses or, when that was not possible, to set up independent Carpatho-Rusyn Orthodox churches.

The American Catholic hierarchy continually tried to enforce Western or Roman practices on their Greek Catholic worshipers—celibacy among priests and the holding of church property by the diocese rather than by a church council of laymen (as was the practice among most early Carpatho-Rusyn churches). When they were pressured too much, individuals and whole parishes were likely to protest by switching their allegiance to the Orthodox church. The most serious division of this kind came in 1929, when the Vatican issued a decree imposing celibacy on all new Greek Catholic priests and abolishing the system whereby laymen owned church property. Several priests and parishes refused to abide by the Vatican decree and in 1937 created instead a new Eastern Christian church, this time in association with the Greek Orthodox rather than the Russian Orthodox church. Now based in Johnstown, Pennsylvania, the new church came to be known as the American Carpatho-Russian Orthodox church. Nearly all its 100,000 members today are of Carpatho-Rusyn background.

These divisions caused much pain within the community, especially during the 1930s and 1940s, a period when parishes, priests, friends, and even families became fiercely divided over religious affiliation. Moreover, the question of who owned existing church buildings and property had to be argued in the Amer-

This view of the Orthodox church in Wilkes-Barre, Pennsylvania, shows the onion-shaped cupolas topped by three-barred crosses that are characteristic of many Eastern Christian churches.

73

ican courts, at the local, state, and federal levels. As the two sides defended themselves in court, they often cited points of history and culture. Ironically, these arguments fostered a new sense of the distinctiveness of Carpatho-Rusyns as an ethnic group. They came to view themselves as different, not only from Roman Catholic Slovaks but also from other Eastern-rite Slavic Christians, such as the Russians and Ukrainians.

The struggle to preserve Carpatho-Rusyn religious traditions in the new American environment took different forms, depending on the church and the time. By the 1950s all churches had begun to replace Church Slavonic (the language of the liturgy) and Carpatho-Rusyn (the language of sermons, confessions, and other individual communications) with English. By 1989 there were only a few parishes that used Church Slavonic and Carpatho-Rusyn alongside English. One of these parishes reaches beyond its immediate neighborhood. An Eastern-rite Catholic mass conducted in Carpatho-Rusyn each Sunday at a church in McKees Rocks, Pennsylvania, a suburb of Pittsburgh, is broadcast live on radio to a large audience.

To the general public, the Carpatho-Rusyn church buildings themselves are certainly the most visible aspect of the group's religious tradition. Some have a ground plan based on the central Greek cross, that is, with transepts running through the main part of the church (the nave) to form a cross of four equal limbs. Others are based on the Western basilica ground plan, in which the nave is longer and one or two towers dominate the western facade, above the front entrance. In either case, Carpatho-Rusyn Orthodox as well as Catholic churches stand out because of their golden domes, often described as onion-shaped cupolas, and because of their three-barred Eastern Christian crosses, on which the bottom transverse piece traditionally sits at an angle to the upright rather than being perpendicular. It is true that the architectural styles brought by Carpatho-Rusyns from Europe are similar to those employed by Ukrainian Americans and Russian Americans. However, one community, the parish of the Byzantine Ruthenian Catholic church in

Roswell, Georgia, recently decided to stress its Old World heritage. In 1982 it built a new church entirely of wood in a style that recalls Carpathian wooden churches in Europe.

Carpatho-Rusyn churches have served not only as spiritual sanctuaries; they have also been and remain centers of community life. Wedding celebrations and other social functions, such as banquets and concerts, are frequently held in church halls. In the early years, at least to the 1940s, many churches, whether Byzantine (Greek) Catholic or Orthodox, also had their own parochial schools where the Carpatho-Rusyn language was taught alongside subjects in English. Some of those schools still exist (in McKeesport and Ambridge, Pennsylvania, and in Joliet, Illinois), and a few even have special programs in Carpatho-Rusyn culture, although all the classes are conducted in English.

Of particular importance in holding the community together is the annual pilgrimage, based on the Old World tradition called the *otpust*. The pilgrimages are held on the grounds of convents and monasteries associated with each of the Carpatho-Rusyn churches, such as the Basilian Convent of Mount St. Macrina near Uniontown, Pennsylvania, affiliated with the Byzantine Ruthenian Catholic church; St. Tikhon's Monastery in South Canaan, Pennsylvania, affiliated with

Left: In Soviet Transcarpathia, the Church of St. Nicholas, at Husnyj, built in 1759. Right: In Roswell, Georgia, the Epiphany Byzantine Ruthenian Catholic Church, built in 1982. Made of wood, the newer church echos many elements of Old World architecture.

In 1905 a group of Russian and Carpatho-Rusyn immigrant families from Mayfield and Jermyn, Pennsylvania, gathered for a weekend pilgrimage at St. Tikhon's Russian Orthodox Monastery in South Canaan, Pennsylvania. This site and others still host many a pilgrimage, or otpust, *for community and religious groups.*

the Orthodox Church in America; and the Monastery of the Ascension in Tuxedo Park, New York, affiliated with the American Carpatho-Russian Orthodox church. The pilgrimages each year draw several thousand participants. Through spiritual renewal, the otpust helps to reinforce the fabric of the Carpatho-Rusyn community.

Pirohi, Prostopinye, and Chardash— Food, Song, and Dance

Of all the traditions brought by the early Carpatho-Rusyn immigrants, food is perhaps the one that has changed the least. Carpatho-Rusyn Americans who in recent years have been able to visit family members in the European homeland are struck by the similarities of their cuisine. The same dishes, such as stuffed cabbage (called either *holubtsi* or *holubki*) with rice or meat, homemade noodles (*halushki*), and stuffed peppers, remain the staples of many Carpatho-Rusyn families, whether in Europe or America, and the liberal use of garlic and sour cream characterizes cooking both in the homeland and in the New World.

In the United States, there have never been any restaurants specializing in Carpatho-Rusyn dishes. Recipes do of course exist, and in 1983, *Gourmet* magazine featured a select number of them in an article about the community's cuisine. Indeed, many Americans, especially in the industrialized Northeast, have come to delight in at least one culinary specialty shared by Carpatho-Rusyns and other East Slavs—*pirohi*. Pirohi are three-cornered wedges of dough (not unlike ravioli) filled with cheese, potatoes, or sauerkraut and covered with sour cream. By selling hundreds of take-out orders of the delectable triangular pirohi, the women's organizations of several Carpatho-Rusyn churches have in recent years helped to raise funds for their parishes as well as expose fellow Americans to Carpatho-Rusyn cuisine.

Certain foods and customs are associated with religious feasts. Easter has always been a major holiday in the Christian calendar, and it is a particularly colorful pageant among Carpatho-Rusyns. Midnight services are still held in most Orthodox churches, and all—Orthodox and Catholic alike—carry out the traditional blessing of post-Lenten Easter baskets at dawn. Those baskets are usually filled with intricately hand-painted Easter eggs (called *pysanky* and *krashanky*) covered with motifs exactly like those done in

A display of festively painted Easter eggs. These two styles of decoration, called pysanky *and* krashanky, *use folk motifs from the European homeland.*

the European homeland. Among the painted eggs of the Slavic groups, the Carpatho-Rusyn eggs are easy to identify: Whereas Ukrainian eggs feature bold geometric lines all around, the Carpatho-Rusyn style relies on patterns of short line strokes or features rustic human and animal figures.

Rusyn-American culture is also noted for its music. The liturgical music for church services that the early immigrants brought with them was easily distinguishable from that of other East Slavs. The Russians and to a lesser degree the Ukrainians have largely depended in their worship on relatively complex choral arrangements sung by a trained choir. Carpatho-Rusyn liturgies, on the other hand, are filled with simple folk melodies invariably sung by the entire congregation. This liturgical plainchant, known as the *prostopinye*, is one of the most distinctive features of Carpatho-Rusyn culture. The prostopinye has been preserved in the Byzantine Ruthenian Catholic church and Carpatho-Russian Orthodox church primarily through oral traditions passed on via the cantor (*diak*), who, after

The choir of St. Mary's Greek Catholic Church, photographed in New York City in 1940. The choristers, all of Carpatho-Rusyn descent, performed at the World's Fair in New York that year.

the priest, is the most important figure in a local parish. The musical memories of individual cantors have been refreshed with recordings made by several church choirs and by cantorial schools and seminars held in recent years. All this activity has gone a long way toward sustaining the art of the plainchant.

Carpatho-Rusyn secular music has also been very popular. It consists of spirited dances like the *chardash* (somewhat similar but distinct from a well-known Hungarian dance) and the more stately *karichka*, as well as jovial or sentimental songs. Many of the songs have lyrics that reflect the difficulties of life in Europe and America, the most well known of which is probably "Chervena ruzha" ("The Red Rose").

In the early years of immigration, such songs and dances were common at baptisms, weddings, and other family gatherings. In recent decades, however, the younger generations have lost much of their knowledge of Carpatho-Rusyn speech, songs, and dances, and the customs have been preserved only in the more formal setting of concerts and recitals by amateur folk ensembles. Several new Carpatho-Rusyn folk ensembles were founded in the 1970s, so the folk culture is by no means disappearing. These ensembles perform regularly at annual ethnic festivals in such places as Pittsburgh and Minneapolis and at the Garden State Festival in New Jersey.

Organizing for Fraternity

Besides the church, the most important unifying feature of Rusyn-American life has been the fraternal or brotherhood organizations. These arose during the very first years of immigration for a simple reason: In the years before social programs such as Social Security or unemployment insurance were enacted, Carpatho-Rusyn and other immigrant workers needed some kind of financial support should they be laid off or injured on the job. The fraternals, then, were a kind of insurance agency for specific ethnic groups to help their members in time of need, whether it be to provide a modest income when members were out of work or to help with burial costs and provide the family with assistance at times of death.

The oldest of the Carpatho-Rusyn fraternal organizations is the Greek Catholic Union, founded in 1892 in the eastern Pennsylvania coal-mining center of Wilkes-Barre. It is still active today. For most of the 20th century, it was based in Pittsburgh or the suburb of Homestead; since 1987 its home has been in Beaver, Pennsylvania, about 30 miles northwest of the city. At the height of its strength, in 1928, the Greek Catholic Union had 120,000 members in more than 1,300 lodges throughout the United States. By the late 1980s membership in the organization stablized at about 50,000 members in 363 lodges. The union remains a successful insurance organization.

The Greek Catholic Union was only one of the many secular fraternal societies established by Carpatho-Rusyns to represent their various religious and political factions and to address their communal needs. Others continue to exist today, including the Russian Orthodox Catholic Mutual Aid Society, the United Societies of Greek Catholic Religion, and the United Russian Orthodox Brotherhood, although their enrollments have dropped to a few thousand members in recent decades.

The fraternals provided more than financial security. They also performed a social and psychological function that at times was just as important to the immigrant. Local lodges sponsored banquets and dances or simply provided a setting where people could meet informally to share their mutual Carpatho-Rusyn language and culture. Most of the fraternals also had women's auxiliaries and youth branches, the latter usually with their own male and female sports teams. By offering such social activities, the fraternals provided a way for immigrants to adapt to American life in a way that allowed them to hold on to what was most crucial to their Carpatho-Rusyn identity. A vivid example is depicted in a popular American film about the Vietnam War, *The Deerhunter* (1978), set in the Carpatho-Rusyn community in Clairton, Pennsylvania, and containing a spirited wedding-party scene that

was filmed in the Lemko Hall in Cleveland, Ohio. (Although the script calls the characters Russians, bits of Rusyn dialect can be heard during that scene.)

In preserving the fabric of the community, the role of the press was all-important. Each of the fraternals had its own press organ, the most important of which was the Greek Catholic Union's *Amerikansky Russky Viestnik* (*American Russian Messenger*). It was launched in 1892 as a weekly and by the 1920s was publishing over 100,000 copies 3 times a week. Since 1952 it has appeared in English as a monthly under the title *Greek Catholic Union Messenger*.

Two banners of the same newspaper illustrate the immigrant community's adaptation to American society. In 1892 (top) the banner was printed in the Carpatho-Rusyn language using the Cyrillic alphabet. By 1941 the language was the same but was in the Latin alphabet. In 1952 the newspaper's name was changed to Greek Catholic Union Messenger, *and since then it has appeared almost entirely in English.*

The newspapers and the fraternals they represented played a crucial role in shaping the direction of Carpatho-Rusyn life in America. They were almost always in the forefront of religious controversies, either defending Greek Catholicism against the policies of the Vatican and the American Catholic hierarchy or trumpeting Orthodoxy as the preferred religious association for Rusyn Americans.

National Realignment, at Home and Abroad

The fraternals and their newspapers were also concerned with politics. Usually this meant not mainstream American politics but Carpatho-Rusyn issues in Europe and America. Indeed, Carpatho-Rusyns were among the few American immigrant groups to have a decisive effect on events in their homeland. After the end of World War I and the dismembering of Austria-Hungary, Rusyn Americans, led by a young Pittsburgh lawyer, Gregory Zhatkovich (son of the founding editor of the *Amerikansky Russky Viestnik*), petitioned President Woodrow Wilson to allow their native land to become an independent country or an autonomous region within a neighboring state. At the urging of the American government, Carpatho-Rusyn immigrant leaders met with Czech and Slovak immigrant spokesmen in America. They then held a meeting in Scranton, Pennsylvania, in late 1918. Among the issues debated were the danger of the Ukrainian language replacing Rusyn in some areas and whether certain counties should be included in Slovakia or the proposed region of Uhro-Rusinia. In the end, the leaders voted to have their homeland annexed as a self-governing region of the new state of Czechoslovakia. This American decision was accepted by the European powers in May 1919. In September of that year the agreement was formalized in the Paris Peace Conference treaty signed at the palace of Saint Germain-en-Laye, just outside Paris.

The other political issue debated at length in the Rusyn-American press was the question of national or ethnic identity. Most immigrants who came to America

identified themselves as Rusnaks or Rusyns, but these terms were unknown in mainstream American society. Moreover, some Carpatho-Rusyns felt that "Rusnak" and "Rusyn" were simply local variants of "Russian," so the group as a whole (especially those who inclined toward Orthodoxy) began to call themselves Carpatho-Russians or simply Russians. Some others argued that Rusyn was either an old name for Ukrainian or that Rusnak was a religious term meaning an Eastern-rite Catholic Slovak.

Together with accompanying religious controversies, the identity issue clouded much of Carpatho-Rusyn life in the United States during the first half of the 20th century. Only since the 1970s have new books and publications helped to resolve the question, and many people of the third, fourth, and fifth generations

Members of the Lemko Association of America and Canada in 1932. The term Lemko *was first used by Carpatho-Rusyns living in Poland who wished to be distinguished from Ukrainians. Some Carpatho-Rusyns continue to use the term.*

The folk ensemble Kruzhok, which means "circle," has members from 13 Rusyn-American church parishes around Cleveland, Ohio. Social clubs and historical societies have also helped revive the ethnic group's cultural awareness since the late 1970s.

are returning to the position taken by the original immigrants: They are describing themselves as descendants of a distinct Slavic culture known as Carpatho-Rusyn.

The most active organization in the recent ethnic revival is the Carpatho-Rusyn Research Center, founded in the midst of the "roots fever" that many groups in the United States caught in the 1970s. Since its establishment in Fairview, New Jersey, in 1978, the new center has published a quarterly cultural magazine, the *Carpatho-Rusyn American*, Rusyn-English phrase books, and scholarly books on Carpatho-Rusyn history and culture. It has sponsored scholarly conferences on Carpatho-Rusyns both in community settings and at American universities, including Harvard, Pennsylvania, Pittsburgh, and John Carroll (in Cleveland, Ohio).

In the same spirit of ethnic revival, descendants of the Carpatho-Rusyn immigrants have also established several new dance ensembles and local cultural clubs. Nor has the language been overlooked. In the late 1970s, Duquesne University in Pittsburgh offered a course in the Carpatho-Rusyn language, and in 1983 a new monthly newspaper in the language, published in Fort Lauderdale, Florida, began to appear.

In the climate of renewed interest in ethnic identity, the churches have reembraced some of the old ways, too, by putting greater emphasis on their Eastern Christian heritage. Many have reinstalled the icon screens (iconostases) that had been taken out during the 1950s and 1960s in the bid to be "more American," and they are offering classes to cantors in the Carpatho-Rusyn prostopinye that has made their liturgies so distinct. These moves testify that whereas the "ethnic fad" has diminished or died out among some groups, for Carpatho-Rusyn Americans it is still flourishing. Interest in their ancestral heritage and the effort to keep it alive through scholarship and popular forms of culture, as well as in the traditional confines of the church, continue to grow.

Joseph M. Gaydos (second from left), a Pennsylvania congressman of Carpatho-Rusyn descent, speaks with President Jimmy Carter (second from right) and others involved in Carter's reelection campaign in 1980.

PEOPLE OF PROMINENCE

Contained within the story of success and achievement of the Carpatho-Rusyn immigrant community as a whole are the stories of individual Carpatho-Rusyn immigrants and, more frequently, the descendants of the first generation who have been able to achieve prominence and obtain positions that enabled them to influence American society as a whole. A few have entered government service, either as elected officials, such as Pennsylvania congressman Joseph M. Gaydos (first elected to office in 1978) and Lieutenant Governor Mark S. Singel (elected in 1968), or as appointed officers, such as George J. Demko, whose title in the Department of State was geographer of the United States. This category also includes Dimitry Zarechnak, who was President Ronald Reagan's translator in negotiations with the Soviet Union, and Orestes J. Mihaly, onetime assistant attorney general of the state of New York. Others have maintained an even higher public profile as entertainers, including Hollywood actress Lizabeth Scott (born as Emma Matzo in 1922), a sultry leading lady of the 1940s and 1950s, and a television actor of partial Carpatho-Rusyn background, Robert Urich, best known as the star of a weekly series about the adventures of a Boston private eye, "Spenser: For Hire." Also in the spotlight in the 1980s was Cora-Ann Mihalik, news anchor for the Fox Television network based in New York City.

From the left: *Soviet premier Mikhail Gorbachev, his translator, President Ronald Reagan, and Dimitry Zarechnak, a State Department diplomatic interpreter of Carpatho-Rusyn descent who served as Reagan's translator at every summit meeting between the two leaders. Photographed here at the White House in October 1986, Zarechnak is one of those Carpatho-Rusyn Americans who have moved into the mainstream of American political life.*

On another level, a few individuals of Carpatho-Rusyn ancestry have left a lasting mark on American life. They include figures from the worlds of entertainment, the arts, music, politics, and religion. Some of them have changed the course of the Carpatho-Rusyn community's life in America or the European homeland; some have acted exclusively in the larger society. It is notable that despite the comparatively great pressure on this small, mostly unknown group to assimilate, its leading figures have managed to preserve their ethnicity. In fact, with one exception, all of the most prominent persons mentioned in this chapter have in some way incorporated their Carpatho-Rusyn heritage into their lifework.

Religion

The Orthodox Church in America is one of the most important Eastern Christian organizations in the United States, and its early growth is largely due to the activity of a Carpatho-Rusyn priest, the Reverend Alexis G. Toth. The American branch of the church actually got its start in the far Northwest, in Alaska, where in the late 18th century Russian colonists were the first Europeans to settle. From that time until 1970, the church organization they carried across the Bering Strait was known as the Russian Orthodox church in America. ("Russian" was then dropped.)

Although it has a long history on the North American continent, the Russian Orthodox church began to grow significantly only at the outset of the 20th century. By then most of its members were not immigrants from Russia but rather East Slavs from the Austro-Hungarian Empire, who worked in the industrial centers of the northeastern and north-central states. The rapid growth in membership in the Russian Orthodox church during those years was due mainly to Toth's missionary work. For his services he is remembered as the Father of Orthodoxy in America.

Alexis G. Toth was born in 1853 in a small Carpatho-Rusyn village in what was then the kingdom of Hungary but is today Czechoslovakia. Like his father, he became a Greek Catholic priest, and in 1880 he was promoted to the post of professor of theology and was named rector of the Greek Catholic seminary in Prešov.

Toth's academic career lasted less than a decade; in 1889 he accepted an invitation from fellow Carpatho-Rusyns living in Minneapolis, Minnesota, to start a new parish there. Soon after his arrival, he reported to the local Roman Catholic bishop at St. Paul. Toth was married, which is permissible for Eastern Catholic priests, but the Roman Catholic church does not accept married priests. The American bishop forbade Toth to perform any clerical duties. Toth persisted, and relations with his superior worsened.

Finally, in March 1891, Toth and his parish decided to break with Rome altogether and to join the Russian Orthodox church. A year later the energetic priest left Minnesota for Pennsylvania, where he proceeded to convert several other Greek Catholic parishes to Orthodoxy. By the time of his death in 1909, Toth had succeeded in bringing at least 20,000 Greek Catholics

The Reverend Alexis G. Toth in the garb of an Orthodox cleric. Toth led a movement to convert Carpatho-Rusyn immigrants in America from the Greek Catholic church to the Russian Orthodox church. The change of alliance enabled Carpatho-Rusyns to maintain their traditional religious practices.

The noted choral director and music arranger Peter Wilhousky wrote the standard concert arrangement for "The Battle Hymn of the Republic." Also a gifted educator, Wilhousky selected and trained the All City High School Chorus of New York, a student choral ensemble that performed annually at Carnegie Hall from 1936 to 1966.

into the Orthodox fold. His missionary work was crucial in that it firmly established Russian Orthodoxy in the United States and moved the faith toward the firm standing it enjoys today, ensuring that its traditions would be preserved in the New World.

Music

Few people realize that when they hear the patriotic anthem "The Battle Hymn of the Republic" or the traditional Christmas song "Carol of the Bells" they are listening to arrangements created by the distinguished choral director and instructor Peter J. Wilhousky.

Wilhousky was born in Passaic, New Jersey, in 1902 into a family of Carpatho-Rusyn origin. His parents had immigrated to America at the beginning of the 20th century from Rusyn villages in what is today the northeastern corner of Czechoslovakia. The young Peter followed in the footsteps of his parents, singing every Sunday in the Passaic Greek Catholic Church. When that parish switched over to Orthodoxy, Peter was sent to the Russian Cathedral Boys Choir in New York City. From there he went on to what was then the Juilliard School of Music and graduated in 1920.

Wilhousky was to make his career in New York City's choral world. He founded the All City High School Chorus in the mid-1930s and taught choral conducting at Juilliard and in master classes in major cities along the East Coast. Many of his students went on to successful careers at the Metropolitan Opera, the New York City Opera, and Radio City Music Hall.

Wilhousky is best known to the public through his stirring and now standard arrangement of "The Battle Hymn of the Republic," which was made especially popular in recordings by the Mormon Tabernacle Choir. (The words were written during the Civil War by Julia Ward Howe and published to great acclaim.) His achievements garnered him numerous awards and accolades during his long life (he died in 1978), and he is remembered by his colleagues and students, and by music lovers in general, as a distinguished educator, gifted arranger, and eminent choral conductor.

Politics

The career of Gregory Zhatkovich provides a sterling example of the close ties between the Carpatho-Rusyn homeland and the United States. Born in Europe in 1886 but raised and educated in America, Zhatkovich was to play a leading role in the political life of his homeland as well as in the advancement of his people in the New World.

When Gregory was five years old, his family moved to Pittsburgh from its native Caraptho-Rusyn village of Holubyne (now in the Soviet Union). The boy's father, Pavel, founded and edited what would become the most important Carpatho-Rusyn commu-

At Independence Hall in Philadelphia in 1919, Gregory Zhatkovich, a Carpatho-Rusyn American, signs the agreement he helped negotiate whereby his family's homeland became the autonomous province of Subcarpathian Rus' in the new nation of Czechoslovakia. His work is one of the best examples of how an immigrant group can affect political events in its homeland.

nity newspaper, the *Amerikansky Russky Viestnik*. In his family's home Gregory learned all about the fate of the Carpatho-Rusyns, who were then living in dire poverty under Hungarian rule in the Hapsburg Empire. These early impressions and the resulting concern for his people back home remained with Zhatkovich even after he received a law degree from the University of Pennsylvania and became a lawyer for General Motors in Pittsburgh.

The chance to act on behalf of his people came unexpectedly with the end of World War I and the collapse of Austria-Hungary in late 1918. Rusyn Americans met several times during that year to discuss the political future of their homeland, and in the fall they chose Gregory Zhatkovich to represent them.

Well versed in American political procedure, the young Zhatkovich—only 32 years old at the time—was able to gain an audience with President Woodrow Wilson in the Oval Office of the White House. The president urged him to meet with Czech and Slovak politicians then in the United States to discuss the possibility that Carpatho-Rusyns in the homeland might join their new state.

Before the end of 1918, Zhatkovich organized a vote among Rusyn Americans. They agreed that their homeland should join the new republic of Czechoslovakia as, in the words of the signed documents, "an autonomous state" or province. The young Rusyn-American spokesman then traveled to Carpathian Rus', where in May 1919 he persuaded local leaders to accept the Czechoslovak solution. They agreed, and the province was named Subcarpathian Rus', indicating that only the portion south of the mountains was included.

Because Zhatkovich was respected in both the United States and the European homeland, in 1920 he was appointed by the Czechoslovak government as the first governor of Subcarpathian Rus'. Zhatkovich, who retained U.S. citizenship, had long ago acquired the American penchant for quick action and political reform, but such boldness did not play well in Central Europe in the unsettled climate of the postwar years. Within a year Zhatkovich resigned in protest because

Gregory Zhatkovich (center) stands before a replica of the Liberty Bell made for the diplomatic meetings in Philadelphia. In 1919 it was presented to the Subcarpathian capital city of Uzhgorod. Zhatkovich, though an American citizen, was the province's first governor.

Czechoslovakia would not immediately grant Carpatho-Rusyns the self-rule they had been promised.

Nevertheless, the decision made by Rusyn Americans to let Czechoslovakia absorb part of their homeland remained in effect, and without question that determination was in large part the work of Gregory Zhatkovich. Many immigrant groups had tried unsuccessfully to enlist the aid of the American government in changing the political boundaries of Europe after World War I; the Carpatho-Rusyns alone were successful. In the words of one historian of those years, Victor S. Mamatey, they represented "a unique case of the influence of an immigrant group in American on the political history of Europe."

Entertainment

In 1978 the motion picture *Grease* took America by storm. Ever since, hundreds of thousands of movie, television, and popular-music fans have enjoyed the many songs and dances in *Grease* that conjured up a nostalgic return to the decade of the 1950s. The film's depiction of the early days of rock and roll and the teenagers in cardigan sweaters and bobby socks who danced and fell in love to its beat helped to usher in America's ongoing love affair with an era it sees as more innocent than the present.

Actress Sandra Dee, born Alexandra Zuck in 1942 to Carpatho-Rusyn parents in Bayonne, New Jersey, poses before filming of the The Restless Years *in 1958.*

What few people know about the movie or the Broadway show that inspired it is that the two main characters were based on real people. One was Sandra Dee, a well-known Hollywood movie star during the late 1950s and early 1960s. On the screen she was played by Olivia Newton-John as a naive and well-mannered teenager who is eventually beguiled by the more flamboyant style of the "super cool" Danny Zucko, played by John Travolta.

The real Sandra Dee was born Alexandra Zuck in 1942 into a Lemko Rusyn family living in Bayonne, New Jersey. (The movie name Danny Zucko surely refers to Sandra Dee's original name.) The blond, blue-eyed Alexandra began her career at the age of 12 as a model for a leading agency in New York City, across the harbor from her hometown. Three years later, in

1957, she acted in her first film, and that same year she signed a long-term contract with United International Pictures in Hollywood.

Within a few years Sandra Dee was known to most moviegoers and was especially popular among the younger set. She seemed always to star as a cute and glamorous nymphet just on the verge of romantic maturity. At least this was the role she played in a string of successful films, among which were *Gidget* (1959), *A Summer Place* (1959), *Tammy, Tell Me True* (1961), and *Take Her, She's Mine* (1963).

By the 1970s, the inexperienced youth was no longer accepted as an accurate representation of teenage Americans, and because she had been typecast in such roles, Sandra Dee's career went into eclipse. Nonetheless, the legend of the beautiful and chaste Sandra Dee was revived in *Grease*, and her character lives on as a symbol of an innocent America.

The Arts

The most widely known American of Carpatho-Rusyn descent was the artist Andy Warhol, whose paintings, films, and photographic creations won him international recognition. Both of his parents came from the Carpatho-Rusyn village of Miková, today located in northeastern Czechoslovakia. His father immigrated to the United States before World War I in search of work; his mother was unable to follow until after the war, in 1921. The second of their three sons was born as Andrew Warhola in Pittsburgh, Pennsylvania, in 1928. (He alone dropped the *a* from the family name.)

Warhol began to draw at a very early age and developed his talent at the Carnegie Institute of Technology in Pittsburgh (now part of Carnegie-Mellon University), where he studied commercial art and fashion illustration. He moved to New York City in 1949 and for nearly a decade worked successfully as a designer of department-store window displays.

Warhol's fascination with the commercial world and with the mass-manufactured products that surround Americans in their daily life led him to choose these subjects for his paintings. In the late 1950s and early 1960s other artists, notably Roy Lichtenstein, were attempting similar fusions of high and low culture; the artistic movement their creations gave rise to became known as pop art. Warhol became one of its most famous practitioners and participants—he reproduced Campbell's soup cans, Coca-Cola bottles, dollar bills, and Brillo boxes on canvas, thereby transforming them from common household objects into art.

Some critics considered this type of reproduction a hoax, and Warhol himself often commented that much of what he did then and later was a joke. Nonetheless, his paintings and prints hang in America's most prestigious museums, including the Museum of Modern Art in New York City and the National Gallery of Art in Washington, D.C. Some historians and critics consider him to have been one of the leading American artists of the second half of the 20th century.

Along with his soup cans and Coca-Cola bottles, Warhol prepared a series of portraits. It seemed to him that television and movies had made the faces of certain public figures as familiar in many homes as soup and soap, so he applied the same technique to them. In 1964 alone, he created studies of Marilyn Monroe, Elvis Presley, Marlon Brando, Elizabeth Taylor, and Jacqueline Kennedy. The impact of these pieces was so great and so immediate that a Warhol rendering became a sort of imprimatur of celebrity; by the end of the 1960s some of America's glitterati wondered if they could retain their fame without a Warhol portrait.

The portraits were made using a silk-screen technique that allows for multiple images to be reproduced, as on a strip of film. Warhol also tried to catch his subjects at their most beautiful and idealized moment. In this sense, the portraits are not at all like household products: They more closely resemble the timeless icons found in Eastern Christian churches, the difference being that Warhol created his icons from the "popular saints" of the 20th century.

By the late 1960s, Warhol had declared that he was a "retired artist," and he began to devote most of his energies to filmmaking. He admitted that his films were simply experiments; most are in fact extremely

long and tedious. They usually focused on the most mundane human activities, as in the case of *Eat* (1963) and *Sleep* (1963), or on problems of sexual relations—*My Hustler* (1965), *Lonesome Cowboys* (1967–68), *Trash* (1971), and *Sex* (1971). Surprisingly, Warhol's films won several awards, and he became a kind of cult figure in the world of underground film. Despite his self-professed retirement, Warhol continued to work. From

Warhol is perhaps best known for his various interpretations of the Campbell's soup can. He painted this version in 1962. By depicting household items on canvas, Warhol seemed to transfigure the mundane into art.

his New York City studio, known as the Factory, he experimented with photography and more portraiture. He also branched out into publishing. Drawing again on the world of glamour and celebrities in which he moved, he founded the monthly magazine *Interview*.

Andy Warhol has been the subject of many books and articles, and he himself wrote three autobiographies. In each of these he always mentioned his Czechoslovak roots, although he never claimed he was of either Czech or Slovak ethnic descent. For the most part he kept his private life a closely guarded secret, so it was only after his unexpected death after a routine surgical procedure in early 1987 that a few details came to the surface. His mother, who was a practicing Byzantine Catholic until her death in 1977, had lived for long periods with Andy in New York City. Warhol, who never married, had throughout his years of international fame retained close ties with his two brothers in Pittsburgh, and he once convinced a nephew not to come to New York but instead to complete his studies at the Byzantine Ruthenian seminary at home. In light of these facts, it is not surprising that his funeral, like his baptism, was held in a Byzantine Catholic church. What is surprising to some people is that Warhol, a man very much part of the secular and flamboyant world of New York fashion and art, never gave up his family or religious ties.

While he lived, Warhol kept in touch with his European relatives in the Czechoslovak part of Carpathian Rus'; his younger brother, who now is a member of the Warhol Foundation, visited the homeland after Andy's death to consider funding a permanent Warhol exhibit in the museum of regional art in Medzilaborce, a town located in the far northeastern corner of Czechoslovakia.

In light of his sometimes outlandish behavior and memorable quotations—it was he who once quipped that in the future everyone will be famous for 15 minutes—Andy Warhol will for many people remain a symbol, a man who exemplified the experimental and often extremist decade of the 1960s. Despite his intense shyness, Warhol always had a superb ability to capitalize on the media and its limitless possibilities for self-projection. Although his ultimate place in art history remains uncertain, his persona continues to fascinate.

The 35th national convention of the Greek Catholic Union, held in Toronto, Ontario, in 1988 proved an occasion to mark the more than 1,100 years that Carpatho-Rusyns have practiced Christianity and the more than 100 years that the community has been a presence in North America.

LOOKING TOWARD THE FUTURE

The nearly 700,000 Americans who can claim one or more forebears of Carpatho-Rusyn origin descend from immigrants who brought very little with them aside from their culture and traditions. Economic hardship forced these immigrants to leave their homeland of Carpathian Rus', for the most part in the three decades before the outbreak of World War I in 1914, a war that destroyed the material and cultural heritage of millions of eastern and central Europeans. In the United States and Canada, thanks to hard work and good fortune, the immigrants' material standards improved substantially. Yet in at least one way the history of these people in America is hauntingly similar to their past in Europe.

The Carpatho-Rusyn homeland has always sat precariously along the borderland of eastern and western Europe. Carpatho-Rusyn culture, tied to the Eastern Christian tradition, was only able to survive by adapting to the Western Christian social and political environment in which it often found itself. The Carpatho-Rusyns' experience with the problems of cultural survival in the European homeland proved invaluable to the immigrants and their descendants in North America. Applying the lessons they had learned about assimilation, they were able to preserve the most crucial ingredients of their identity. As Rusyn Americans, they generally replaced their spoken language with English; some of their churches were obliged to give up particular Carpatho-Rusyn traditions; and some of the American-born generations lost or grew uncertain of their specific ethnic identity. Considering the difficult situation, it is noteworthy that these various active and passive means of adaptation never led to complete assimilation in the sense of losing all memory of a distinctive Carpatho-Rusyn heritage.

Most descendants of Carpatho-Rusyns still live in or near the towns and cities of the northeast and north-central industrial belt where their immigrant ancestors first settled. Their oldest and largest fraternal society, the Greek Catholic Union, remains a well-run organization that on the eve of its centenary in 1992 is proud of a trend of slow but steady growth. Their churches, be they Greek Catholic or Orthodox, attract a steady number of people, who find there a focal point for both religious worship and community events (banquets, dances, and bingo nights) and family celebrations (weddings and anniversaries).

Anybody in the Carpatho-Rusyn community over the age of 15 has witnessed or been a part of a decided upsurge in cultural awareness—what some participants have called a Rusyn renaissance. This renaissance began in earnest during the mid-1970s, when "roots fever" and the American bicentennial celebrations cast a spotlight on the contributions of immigrant groups and ethnic cultures to the American nation. Like other groups, Carpatho-Rusyn Americans joined in the search for their past. They, too, wished to stand up and be counted.

The search took the form of several activities. Over a dozen folk ensembles have been founded in various communities, each dedicated to performing authentic Carpatho-Rusyn songs and dances from the homeland. Some of the churches, such as the Greek Catholic

ones that had given up many of the Old World traditions, have undergone a spiritual revival that stresses a renewal of their Eastern Christian heritage by purifying the liturgy of Western influences, by restoring iconostases and Eastern Christian decorative elements inside the churches, and by building new houses of worship that either draw on traditional architectural motifs—such as St. Mary's Catholic Church of the Byzantine Rite in New York City—or revive the Carpathian wooden style, as was done in Roswell, Georgia. This resurgence promises to continue well into the 1990s.

Such activity has gone hand in hand with a new concern for the history of the group and has sparked much cultural-preservation work. The founding of the Heritage Museum in West Paterson, New Jersey, in the 1970s and the Archdiocesan Museum in Pittsburgh are examples. Both of these museums already house some of the largest collections of printed materials and religious and secular paintings and relics from Carpathian Rus' to be found in North America.

The renaissance has been bolstered by extensive scholarly research about the life of Carpatho-Rusyns in Europe and North America. Some of North America's leading publishers have issued books and articles

The Slavjane Folk Ensemble of McKees Rocks, Pennsylvania. Since the 1970s several such groups have revitalized Carpatho-Rusyn dancing and singing.

Bishop Michael J. Dudick of the Greek Catholic diocese of Passaic, New Jersey, has helped amass a collection of art, folk costumes, and other items for the Rusyn-American Heritage Museum in West Paterson.

about the group that have been sold widely within the community with the help of some churches, fraternal organizations, and in particular the Carpatho-Rusyn Research Center. Many of these books have even appeared in second and third editions, a sure sign that interest is expanding. To complement the folk ensembles, church renewal, and scholarly activity, there have been adult-education classes organized to teach the Carpatho-Rusyn language, cantorial leadership, Easter-egg painting, and ethnic cooking.

Success in two realms has made Americans of Carpatho-Rusyn descent ready to learn about the heritage of their ancestors. One is economic assimilation, which makes them materially able. The other is cultural adaptation, which leaves them psychologically prepared. For the first time, the existence of publications, research, and community organization affords all Rusyn Americans the chance to proudly share in their religious and cultural traditions. Knowledge about the group, once again within reach, seems assured for future generations as well.

"All things considered," concludes a recent editorial comment on Carpatho-Rusyns in America by cultural activist John Righetti, "it seems remarkable that several tens of thousands of poor, often illiterate immigrants arriving in America before World War I have produced offspring who several generations later, and several thousand miles from the European homeland, still in some way retain a sense of Carpatho-Rusyn identity." It is indeed remarkable, and the same qualities that have enabled Carpatho-Rusyn immigrants and their descendants to prosper make it likely that their community in America will enjoy a bright future.

FURTHER READING

Barriger, Lawrence. *Good Victory: Metropolitan Orestes Chornock and the American Carpatho-Russian Orthodox Greek Catholic Diocese.* Brookline, MA: Holy Cross Orthodox Press, 1985.

Davis, Jerome. *The Russians and Ruthenians in America: Bolsheviks or Brothers?* New York: George H. Doran, 1922.

McWilliams, Tatyana. "A Ruthenian Heritage." *Gourmet*, April 1983.

Magocsi, Paul Robert. *Our People: Carpatho-Rusyns and Their Descendants in North America.* 2nd ed. Toronto: Multicultural History Society of Ontario, 1985.

————. *The Shaping of a National Identity: Subcarpathian Rus', 1848–1948.* Cambridge: Harvard University Press, 1978.

————, ed. *Wooden Churches in the Carpathians: The Photographs of Florian Zapletal.* Vienna: Wm. Braumüller, 1982.

Markovyč, Pavlo. *Rusyn Easter Eggs from Eastern Slovakia.* Vienna: Wm. Braumüller, 1987.

Osborn, Kevin. *The Ukrainian Americans.* New York: Chelsea House, 1989.

Roccasalvo, Joan. *The Plainchant Tradition of Southwestern Rus'.* Boulder, CO, and New York: Columbia University Press for the *East European Quarterly*, 1986.

Roman, Michael, ed. *Jubilee Almanac of the Greek Catholic Union of the U.S.A.* Munhall, PA: Greek Catholic Union, 1967.

Simirenko, Alex. *Pilgrims, Colonists, and Frontiersmen: An Ethnic Community in Transition.* New York: Free Press, 1964.

Tarasar, Constance J., and John H. Erickson, eds. *Orthodox America, 1794–1976.* Syosset, NY: Orthodox Church in America, 1975.

Warzeski, Walter. *Byzantine Rite Rusins in Carpatho-Ruthenia and America.* Pittsburgh: Byzantine Seminary Press, 1971.

INDEX

PICTURE CREDITS

PAUL ROBERT MAGOCSI is a professor of history and political science at the University of Toronto, where he holds the Chair of Ukrainian Studies. He is the author of *The Russian Americans* for the Chelsea House PEOPLES OF NORTH AMERICA series, and his many other publications include *The Shaping of a National Identity: Subcarpathian Rus', 1848–1948; Galicia: A Historical Survey and Bibliographical Guide; Our People: Carpatho-Rusyns and Their Descendants in North America;* and *Ukraine: A Historical Atlas.* He has also served as research editor, map editor, and author of several entries in the *Harvard Encyclopedia of American Ethnic Groups.*

DANIEL PATRICK MOYNIHAN is the senior United States senator from New York. He is also the only person in American history to serve in the cabinets or subcabinets of four successive presidents— Kennedy, Johnson, Nixon, and Ford. Formerly a professor of government at Harvard University, he has written and edited many books, including *Beyond the Melting Pot, Ethnicity: Theory and Experience* (both with Nathan Glazer), *Loyalties,* and *Family and Nation.*